Louise Robinson Chapman
On Assignment from God

by
Helen F. Temple

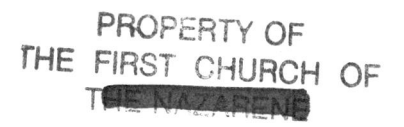

Nazarene Publishing House
Kansas City, Missouri

Copyright 1993
by Nazarene Publishing House

ISBN: 083-411-4720

Printed in the
United States of America

Cover Design: Royce Ratcliff

Unless otherwise indicated, all Scripture quotations are from the King James Version of the Bible.

Quotations marked NIV are taken from the *Holy Bible, New International Version®* (NIV®). Copyright © 1973, 1978, 1984 by International Bible Society. Used by permission of Zondervan Publishing House. All rights reserved.

10 9 8 7 6 5 4 3 2 1

Helen Temple served as editor of the World Mission Division for 32 years. She has authored 37 adult and 8 children's missionary reading books. Recent titles include *Thy Bread and Water Shall Be Sure* and *To Live Is Christ*.

Miss Temple is a graduate of Eastern Nazarene College (A.B., Th.B.). She also holds an M.A. in English from Boston University. Prior to her tenure in the World Mission Division, she served as Church Schools editor in the junior and teens department.

Miss Temple resides in Olathe, Kans., where her leisure is invested in gardening, quilting, and reading.

Contents

Foreword	7
Preface	9
1. The Early Years	11
2. College and the Covenant	21
3. To Africa	32
4. "Not Go Back"	41
5. It Is for the World	49
6. The Challenges Multiply	57
7. Assignment to the World	66
8. A Dream Fulfilled—and Catastrophe	74
9. A New Assignment—Again?	79
10. "God's Pet" Receives Her Last Assignment	88

Foreword

One of my earliest recollections as a child was hearing Dr. Louise Chapman preach about holiness, missions, prayer, and soul winning—the focuses of her ministry.

In 1983, while I was serving as district NWMS president of South Carolina, Dr. Chapman was the district convention speaker. It was then that she and I became bonded as mother and daughter in Christ. Dr. Chapman began nurturing me in the deeper things of God and in leadership strategies. Often she has said to me, "Daughter, remember, we are on assignment from God." She prayed me, she said, to the position of general NWMS director and has prayed daily for my ministry ever since.

We have spent many hours sharing the exciting work God is doing all over the world, reviewing mission programs, and discussing future projects. I, along with thousands of others throughout the world, have sought her wise counsel repeatedly.

With interest, I listened to every response Dr. Chapman gave in her 100th birthday celebration, October 9, 1992. It was obvious that, even though it was a historical event, her focus was on the harvest and not on the history.

Dr. Chapman has lived in tune with God. Before she went to the throngs, she went to the throne. Before she tackled the challenges, she talked with the Christ.

Ferdinand Foch said that the greatest force on earth is "the human soul on fire." Dr. Louise Chapman is a soul on fire. Her passion is contagious to all generations. I commend *Louise Robinson Chapman—On Assignment from God* to you from the pen of renowned reading book author Helen Temple.

—NINA G. GUNTER
General NWMS Director

Dr. Louise Robinson Chapman on her 99th birthday, October 9, 1991

Preface

Trying to put the life and spirit of Louise Robinson Chapman on paper is like harnessing electricity—a lot more escapes you than what you capture.

Louise Chapman is a great woman—by the grace of God a humble, holy woman—and an intensely human one.

It has been a faith-building experience to trace her life from the timid young girl who was terrified at saying grace at the table to the homebound saint who enthusiastically undertakes to raise a million dollars for "God's radio" in her 99th year.

What an example for Christians anywhere on the journey to heaven, who have not yet dared to serve God with reckless abandon! Hopefully, as you read this, you will catch a glimpse of what you are missing.

Louise candidly admits, "Sometimes it takes months for me to be sure that a new project is the will of God, but once I know, I never hesitate. I begin at once to do it."

I am grateful to Louise's sisters, Josephine and Florence, now deceased, who earlier shared memories of their childhood and youth growing up with Louise.

Many thanks also to those who responded to my request for accounts of Louise's ministry to them during these later, homebound years. Thank you for your letters and tapes. Be assured that someone, reading your stories, will take heart and try again.

And special thanks to Louise, who entrusted me with the story of her life-transforming journey with God.

When we asked Louise's permission to tell her story she said, a little reluctantly, "Well, all right, if it will win some souls, and perhaps give a few more people a vision for the ministry of World Mission Radio."

With her wish in mind, I offer you this book. May God speak through its pages.

TRANSVAAL
• Sabie

REPUBLIC OF SOUTH AFRICA

• Endingeni

Komati River

MOZAMBIQUE

• Manzini
(formerly Bremersdorp)

Usutu Forest

Great Usutu River

SWAZILAND

1

The Early Years

"I'm concerned about Louise," Mother Robinson sighed. "She doesn't seem able to learn."

"What makes you think that?" Father Robinson said, frowning. "She seems smart enough to me."

"I know," Mother Robinson agreed, pushing the darning egg into another sock. "But when the teacher gives out lessons, Louise forgets to bring her book home, or she says she doesn't know what the teacher wants."

"Lula is such a quick learner; I can't understand Louise."

"Talk to her. Find out what her trouble is." Father dismissed the subject with a shrug.

Stopping Louise when the other children were busy outside, Mother Robinson tried again to fathom her second daughter's difficulty.

"Louise, what is your homework assignment tonight?" she asked cheerily.

"Don't have any," Louise answered, edging away from her mother.

"No homework?" Mother pretended surprise. "Didn't the teacher tell you to study anything for tomorrow?"

"I didn't hear her say anything."

"Did you ask her?"

Louise looked at her mother startled. "No ma'am. Not her!"

"What do you mean?" Mother Robinson asked, gently relentless.

"She's MEAN!" Louise exploded. "Nobody asks her anything!"

"Well, did you ask one of the other pupils?"

"No use." Louise was wiggling now, trying to escape. "She'll give me a zero anyway. She doesn't like me."

Mother Robinson sighed and let the child go. Whatever the reason was, she realized she would not learn it from Louise.

For the rest of the year, Louise reluctantly followed her brother and sister to the little one-room school and endured the scoldings that daily fell upon her small shoulders.

Not for the world would she confess to her mother that she was terrified of the stern teacher who wielded her rod freely over the hapless students.

The next year, a new teacher appeared at Oakdale School and to everyone's surprise, Louise suddenly began to learn, moving rapidly to the head of her class.

Before Louise finished grammar school, the family moved to Ridgefield, Wash., where Louise completed grade school. She then went on to Ridgefield High School, boarding with a family in town. While in high school, she took teacher training classes and began teaching before she had graduated. The little grade school tomboy had become a pretty, vivacious teenager, never lacking an escort to the country dances and parties.

During Louise's third year of high school, Father Robinson bought a 150-acre farm in View, Wash. In the middle of the year, Louise went to visit her family there. Lula had begun to attend a little church in View—a source of amusement and amazement to her brothers and sisters, for the family had never been interested in religion.

"Come with me tonight," Lula invited when Louise arrived. "Some Scandinavian boys are singing in the meetings. They are handsome! Good singers too!"

Louise agreed to go on Friday night. The singing and special music went on for 45 minutes before the preacher began to talk. Surrounded by other young people, the evening passed quickly. Louise was surprised to discover that she liked church.

She went with Lula again on Sunday evening. The church was full when they arrived. There was no place to sit with the young people in the back, so they sat close to the front among the older saints. During the singing, Grandma Hansen got blessed and began to jump up and down, praising the Lord as hairpins flew out and her white hair cascaded down her back. Louise was disgusted. "That silly old fool," she fumed. "How can she act like that?"

Down the row of seats from Grandma sat Mother Courtney, looking up toward the ceiling with a sweet smile on her face. Louise stared at the ceiling. There was nothing there. What was the woman smiling about?

Suddenly, without warning, the Lord spoke to Louise: "If you had what she has, you, too, could smile."

A wave of conviction swept over Louise. She was gripped by a strange longing to have whatever it was that made those two women so happy.

Almost in the same moment came the realization that there were apologies to be made and wrongs to make right if she was ever to have that kind of joy.

She recalled the blouse tucked in the back corner of her dresser. She had found it in the attic of the home where she had lived the year before. She had worn it once, intending to return it, but did not go back to that home and still had the blouse. She knew she would have to return the blouse somehow, but how could she explain having kept it so long?

The price for joy seemed intolerably high. Louise rebelled at the thought of embarrassing herself by asking forgiveness of others for sharp words she had spoken.

She went back to high school on Monday, miserable with conviction, afraid to go to sleep at night lest she wake up in hell. She tried to pray. God said He would help her if she would make the restitution and apologies.

Her proud heart rebelled. "I can't do it," she argued. "It is an impossible thing You ask."

Her conscience told her that if she didn't do it, she would have to go to hell.

Every time she closed her eyes, Louise felt she was sliding down into God's punishment.

In an agony of distress, Louise promised she would do all that God asked if He would let her get back to the little church where people knew how to pray.

She tried to reach her brother Frank to ask him to come and get her. Before she made contact with him, he appeared on Friday and asked if she would like to come back to View with him. Suddenly, she didn't want to go, but she was afraid not to do it.

Arriving home, she discovered there was a revival in a schoolhouse in Diamond Hill Grove, 10 miles from the farm. Louise went with the others, joining the young people in the back seats of the church.

At the invitation to come and pray, she walked out instantly, fearing that God would strike her dead if she delayed her response. She knelt at the altar. Someone told her to pray.

"I don't know how to pray," she admitted.

"Then repeat the words after me," the voice instructed.

She did. As she finished, she stood up. "It's all right," she said.

She didn't feel any different, but she believed that God kept His word, and there was no need to linger there.

She walked home with a crowd of the young people.

Even as she listened to their chatter, she heard God speak. "Louise, stay home. Do not go back to school."

"All right," she replied, "I'm a Christian now. I'll do as You say."

The next morning, as she washed clothes over a scrub board in the backyard, she sang a song that she had learned the night before: "Oh, the joy of sins forgiv'n! / Oh, the bliss the Blood-washed know! / Oh, the peace akin to heav'n, / Where the healing waters flow!"

Suddenly, the glory of God swept over her. She wept and shouted praise to God. So this is what it is like to be a Christian, she thought, assuming that this kind of glory would be there from then on.

There was much work to be done on a large farm. Cherries, apples, pears, plums, and grapes covered several acres. Wild blackberries were abundant. The Robinson children worked together to harvest the fruit. At blackberry picking time, they went out for the day, scattering over the fields where the berries grew. One day, the boys heard faint yells from a distant field. When the calls continued, Henry went to investigate. He found Florence and Josie down in an abandoned, dry well. It had been covered over with brush and as they stepped on the pile to reach for berries, they had plunged to the bottom. Laughing at their predicament, he leaned down and helped them out.

In a good season they often canned as many as 700 quarts of blackberries for winter use.

With 18 kinds of apples, 6 kinds of plums, plus grapes and cherries, the harvest season lasted all summer and fall.

Always, there was a large "house" garden of tedious rows of beans, corn, cucumbers, rutabagas, potatoes, carrots, and other root vegetables to be hoed, weeded, and harvested at the right time.

In addition to their own crops, the Robinson children found time to work for neighboring farmers to earn a little cash. When the spring salmon runs began in the river, the boys dipped salmon to salt or smoke or eat fresh.

Nothing edible was ignored. Even the youngest children learned where to find wild dandelions, pigweed, woolly britches, and wild mustard. These became welcome additions to the vegetable and fruit crops.

Between farm chores there was time for fun. The

young people gathered at each other's homes for taffy pulls, charades, or singing around the piano.

Solitude was a rare thing in a family of eight children. Louise found a spot in the pasture where three fir trees had fallen to form a triangle. Seedlings had grown up between the fallen trees, creating a green sanctuary. Here, she would come to read the Bible and pray. And here God began to speak to Louise through visions. This gift was shared by Louise's father, who often foresaw events before they happened.

One day, as Louise was praying in her private "chapel," she heard people going down the path. She looked out through the trees and saw a tunnel of concrete and on it a throng of people rushing along as though driven. She ran with them, until she saw them falling over the edge of a precipice into the flames of hell. She leaned over and tried to stop them but couldn't. She ran back to the pasture, where Jesus was standing.

"Don't You see what's happening, Jesus?" she cried. "Why don't You stop them?"

"You stop them," He replied.

"I can't! I've tried. They won't listen."

Jesus wrapped her in a white veil and a fire began to burn in her heart. Jesus put her down by the road. "Now you stop them," He said.

She called out to the running crowd that hell was ahead. People listened. She pulled them off the concrete tunnel and pushed them on a shining path that led up to heaven.

As the vision faded, Louise wondered what it meant. God seemed to be telling her that people everywhere needed to be rescued from their lives of sin. But how?

God was beginning the training of His young recruit. It was steady, relentless, and always ahead of where she was comfortable in her Christian life.

While Louise was still a very new Christian, the pastor of the little church tried unsuccessfully to raise $7.00 to pay on the church mortgage. No one seemed to have any money to give, and Louise left the church heavyhearted. As she prayed about it, God told her to go back the next Sunday and raise the whole $27.00 needed to pay the mortgage in full. "And I want you to give $1.00 of it," He said.

"Where would I get a dollar?" Louise cried. "I haven't had any cash for months. And please don't ask me to stand up in front of those people and ask them to give. They don't have any cash either. They won't listen to me. I'm the youngest Christian there."

God held her to His assignment. She tried to get the church board members to do it. They insisted there was no use to try. She prayed to be sick so that she would not have to go to church Sunday. She awakened well and strong.

The pastor tried again to raise the $7.00 needed for the payment overdue. No one responded. Trembling, Louise stood and told the people what God had told her to do, then burst into tears. Farmers dug into their pockets and gave $26.00—almost the total amount owed. Only Louise's dollar remained to be paid. After the morning service, the pastor asked Louise to take a group of young people to Diamond Hill that afternoon and have a testimony meeting.

It was Louise's first time to lead a meeting. The young people sang and shouted and praised God. The old farmers clapped and enjoyed the service. At the close, Louise remembered that the pastor usually stood at the door after church and shook hands as people left. She went to the door and stood. An elderly Christian man came past, shook hands, and left a silver dollar in her hand. Forgetting all about shaking hands, Louise started for home to pay her pledge to the church.

With this first lesson in obedience completed, God immediately presented another.

Within a few weeks of her conversion, a preacher visited the little church and preached on saying grace at the table and having a family altar.

God said, "Louise, go home and do that. Start saying grace at each meal, and begin to have a family altar."

Louise was horrified. "Lord, You know I couldn't do that. My father wouldn't let me. You mustn't ask me to do such hard things. You have to be reasonable."

And God replied, "But I want you to."

Louise's heart filled with rebellion. She put her face down in the straw by the altar. "Lord, I want You and I love You, but You do ask me to do such hard things. If I could always live with my head in the straw, then maybe I could do these hard things, but I don't see how."

Finally, with a glimmer of faith, she said, "If You will help me, Lord, probably I could do it."

Tears of surrender flowed, until, in a trembling voice, she whispered, "I'll start tomorrow morning."

After a fear-filled, sleepless night, Louise crept from bed, ready to obey God.

Immediately everything went wrong. Before the family reached the breakfast table her father became fiercely angry over something.

Louise cried in silent anguish, "Lord, this is no time to start. I shouldn't have said I'd do it this morning."

The family began to gather in the kitchen. Louise ran to a dark cubbyhole under the stair. "O God, help me!" she wailed. "Help me!"

She felt a strong, invisible arm around her. Strength began to flow through her spirit.

She went to the table, sat down with the others, and said in a trembling voice, "Father, may I return thanks?"

Surprisingly calm, her father replied, "I don't mind if my children are Christians, if they aren't hypocrites."

Louise said grace. The meal began silently, but soon her father began to lecture about the hypocrites he'd known in his life.

After breakfast, Louise said softly, "Would you come into the living room and let me pray with you?"

Her father pushed back his chair and stomped out to the barn. The boys went out on the porch, shaking their heads and laughing. The girls giggled. Mother Robinson went in and sat on the couch. Louise sat down on the piano stool wondering what to do. Just then Father Robinson came striding back to the house. He threw his hat into the corner and said, "Come on, boys!" The family gathered in self-consciously and sat down.

"Go on," Father said, looking sternly at Louise.

She picked up the Bible and it fell open at John 14. She read the first verse and burst into tears.

Silently the family slipped out of the room and left her alone. She ran upstairs and flung herself on the bed, weeping. "I told You I couldn't do it," she cried.

"But you did," God reminded her. "Tomorrow it will be easier."

Painfully, Louise kept on with family devotions and grace at meals. And before that summer ended, Mother and Father Robinson were converted at a camp meeting and, a few weeks later, her two sisters also were saved.

The Robinson home took on a different aura. Church became central in their lives, even though the boys did not follow the others immediately in accepting Christ.

Church families often gathered in one another's homes after the morning service. Each family brought food baskets, and tables were set up under the fruit trees. The next Sunday, the families went to another home to eat and fellowship together.

Sometimes, even during the busy weekdays, the Robinsons would see friends coming down the road in wagons. Often this meant an overnight visit with hymn singing around the piano.

On one occasion, Louise and Florence dressed in pretty, white dresses and did their hair in a fancy style to go to a young people's party at a friend's house. It was a long distance around by the road, but much closer if they cut across the neighbor's pasture. They decided to try the pasture, since there seemed to be only a few cows in sight.

Halfway across the pasture, they heard the neighbor's bull bellow and saw him galloping toward them. They ran for the nearest tree. Florence scrambled up first, with Louise close behind.

"Get up higher!" Louise yelled, peering down at the snorting bull.

"I can't," Florence answered. "I'm up with the birds now."

The angry bull pawed the ground under the tree and butted it with his head. Around the tree he circled, looking up at the frightened girls. For an hour they clung to their perch, terrified that the animal would shake them out of their refuge.

Finally, the bull decided they were not going to move, and he wandered away. When he was out of sight, Louise and Florence crept down the tree, hurried to a ravine, and ran toward the fence in the distance. They were nearly there when they heard the bull bellowing again and saw him coming toward them. They raced for the fence, stumbling over the rough ground. Florence reached it first, climbed on a log, and went over the top. Louise flung herself on the ground and rolled under the fence just ahead of the horns of the angry bull. Shaken, they stood up and looked at each other. Their white dresses were crumpled and smeared with dirt. Their hair had come loose and was streaming down their backs. There was no way they could go to the party looking as they did. They walked to a farmer's house and cleaned up the best they could. It was too late to walk home. They stayed all night and returned home the next day.

2

College and the Covenant

Even before she completed high school, Louise took a teaching position in a little country school in Lucia Falls. She rode a pony 30 miles, rain or shine.

Sunday afternoons Louise often took a group of young people from the church to a rural school for services. They sang, testified, prayed, and usually one of the group gave a little talk. It was a pleasant life, filled with warm fellowship, friends, and the dream of a future as a teacher.

Yet, deep in her heart, Louise was convinced that God had a different plan for her life. How or where to find it, she was not sure.

She stood one day under the big cherry tree by her grandmother's door. Looking up into its leafy branches, she pondered what to do. Schools were asking her to come and teach. Should she accept one of these as God's plan?

Out of her thoughts, she heard the Voice she had come to know and love.

"Louise, lovest thou Me more than these?"

In a rush of sentiment, Louise's thoughts swept over the warm Christian love and fellowship of family and church friends; the familiar activities at home and church; the joy she found in teaching—all dear and familiar things that she loved.

The Voice spoke again: "Louise, lovest thou Me more than these?"

She answered honestly, "No, Lord, I don't. But I wish I did."

God said, "Feed My sheep."

She knew then that she must go to school and prepare for whatever God wanted her to do. But where?

She thought of Pasadena College in California, but she knew she did not have the money to pay her way.

Northwest Nazarene College was closer, and she had heard that students could work for their school expenses there.

In her typical persuasive enthusiasm, Louise talked two neighbor girls and her sister Florence into going to NNC with her.

None of them had the funds to pay for their education. They had the price of a train ticket and a few dollars extra. But they were full of hope and expectancy for obtaining work to help them through college.

In their ignorance, they did not think of writing ahead to tell the school when they would arrive. They reached Nampa very early in the morning—too early to call anyone. Not knowing what to do, they huddled in the cold train station and waited for dawn. Leaving the others sitting with their luggage, Louise and one of the other girls walked out into the moonlight to see what the town of Nampa, Idaho, looked like. They had never seen irrigation ditches, and their first glimpse of the water-filled ditch shining in the moonlight looked like a sidewalk. A few steps at the edge quickly revealed their mistake.

When it was daylight, they found a battered telephone book and ran their anxious fingers down the pages in search of a familiar name.

The H's brought success with Rev. Harry Hays who had held a revival in their church some time before. They called him and told him they had come to go to college.

Rev. Hays went to the station, picked up the weary, hungry girls, and took them to his home for breakfast and a place to rest. Before the day was over, the girls fanned out in the town, looking for work. Florence found a position in a well-to-do home. The other girls also found housework positions. For Louise, there seemed to be nothing.

But God was taking the long view. He knew the training Louise needed for His future assignment.

That evening, Rev. Hays said, "I've been looking for a yard boy. Would you want to try that?"

Desperate, Louise accepted the job. While the other girls cleaned, cooked, and dusted in homes, Louise milked cows, cleaned the milk separator and the barn, and maintained the yard. It paid her room and board for the first semester. The next semester she found easier work and moved.

She knew she had a long stretch of preparation ahead of her. Before she could even enroll in college, she had to complete her high school credits.

Eager to prepare for God's calling, she plunged in, working at any task that came her way. She soon became known as an able substitute teacher, and before long had taught classes for every professor there. Penmanship classes became a regular assignment. One year, Louise was matron of the high school girls' dormitory. Another year, she managed the college dining room, planned meals, and bought the food supplies.

President H. Orton Wiley noted her activity and vowed that he was going away some day and let her be president of the college for a day.

For a time, Louise and Florence earned money serving banquets. Louise prepared the food; Florence managed the dining hall. Pinching and scrimping, doing without all but the bare necessities, Louise reached her junior year of college. Then her money completely ran out. Her dress had been patched almost beyond any possibility of further patching. Her shoes were scrubby and worn. She had nothing for books or tuition.

Desperate, she got excused from her work and walked the several miles back to her room to talk to God.

"Lord," she prayed tearfully, "I'm at the end. I can't go on any longer. I have to quit school and go to work to earn some money."

God said, "What do you need?"

"I need books, underclothes, tuition. I only have one dress."

"What do you need today?"

"Tuition."

"You don't need that until next week."

"I need a history book."

"Don't you have three or four dollars in your trunk?"

"Yes, but it's not mine. I borrowed it, and I have to pay it back."

"You could buy the history book with it. The man you owe isn't here right now."

"I need clothes."

"Didn't you patch yesterday?"

"Yes, but it's patch on patch. In two days I'll need to do it again."

"That's not today."

Louise gave up and went dejectedly back to work. She waited stubbornly until her tuition was overdue, her clothes torn and threadbare. Then she went home again to pray.

God did not come in answer to her call.

"Lord," she prayed in despair, "when You said I could wait, You came. When I need You, You don't answer. What will I do?"

Silence was her only response.

That night, as she studied late on her Greek, she felt a presence in the room. She turned around quickly and saw Jesus standing behind her. He said, "You've been calling me?"

"Yes, I need money," Louise responded. "All the students have parents and friends to help them. I have no one. I'm in such desperate condition I have to quit school and earn some money."

Jesus came to the table and held out His hands full of gold. He said, "I could give you someone to help. I'll give you money. Take it. I hadn't planned to do it that way. I sent you here. I intended to pay your bills. If you want someone else, I can give you someone else. But if you will put Me and My kingdom first, and trust Me, I'll supply all your needs."

Louise burst into tears at her lack of faith. When she looked up from her weeping, Jesus was gone. Her heart burned within her for days. She clasped His covenant to her secret heart and began to trust God for every need. The covenant Jesus gave her that night became the foundation of her life: God first—always, and trust Him to decide what she needed and to supply it.

She returned to classes, holding fast to the covenant, and God began to pay her bills.

There were days of crisis at Northwest Nazarene College as in most of the Nazarene colleges. At one time, the college was desperately in need of $25,000. Students and faculty were poor, and few were able to give much money. As the president pleaded with people to help raise the needed funds, Louise thought, If Dr. Winchester were here, I'd ask her to give $500.

God said, "Louise, you pledge $500."

"You can't be serious, Lord," she answered. "I don't even have $5.00."

"If Dr. Winchester asked you to pledge $500 for her, would you do it?"

"Of course, Lord. I'd do my best."

"Can't you trust Me to help you give $500?"

"Yes, I guess I can," she admitted.

Louise was sitting in the choir as she silently talked with God. That night, she sat down near the front in the congregation. She wrestled with the audacity of pledging $500 when she could not get even $5.00 for school needs.

By the third service, she sat near the back, but the struggle went on.

Slowly the pledges crept toward $12,000. People were going to the front and writing on the blackboard the amount they would give. Trembling, Louise walked to the front and wrote $500 on the board. Tears were streaming down her cheeks as she returned to her seat. People knew her financial circumstances. They were blessed and excited by her step of faith. One after another they began pledging. The offering went far over the $25,000 goal. The whole congregation was blessed by Louise's obedience.

As the pledges mounted, God said, "This is a gift from Me. The gift of raising money. Use it for Me and My kingdom." In small, sacrificial amounts through the rest of the year, God enabled Louise to pay her pledge.

During Louise's junior year in college, she came upon thousands of bleating sheep along the side of the road as she walked to class. She looked at them and they seemed like lost souls without any shepherd. Overwhelmed, she dropped to her knees beside the ditch and wept. Her mind was filled with a vision of millions of Chinese, Spanish, and Africans. How long she knelt there, she did not know, but she carried the vision heavy on her heart for days.

Often after that experience, she had a repeated vision of a dark-skinned man walking back and forth on top of the mountains, with his arms out toward America. He called and called for help. Louise went to see what he wanted. She tried to climb the cliff but couldn't. Skinned and bruised, with torn clothing, she climbed as high as she could. Then a great hand came down over the cliff and lifted her up. She followed the Man of the Mountain into the heart of Africa.

Louise was troubled by this recurring vision. What did it mean? She could not go to all these countries. What was God asking her to do?

Finally, Louise locked herself in her room. "I'm not leaving this room until I settle my call and know what God wants," she vowed.

Kneeling beside her bed she prayed, "Lord, You know how I've tried to obey You. I don't understand these visions. I don't know what You want me to do."

God said, "Will you preach?"

"Lord, that's the same question we've debated for two or three years. You're God. You do what is right. I'm going to preach until You tell me You don't want me to anymore. I'm not a preacher. You know that. I'll preach and disgrace You until You'll be glad to release me."

"What about the fellow you're engaged to?"

Desperate, Louise surrendered. "I'll break my engagement until You say to go on."

"Will you preach in Africa?"

In a flash, Satan reminded Louise of missionary women she had seen with long black dresses and funny shoes, their hair in an untidy knot on top of their heads. From all she had heard, they lived in near starvation, sitting on a cracker box in front of some African home, telling Bible stories to children.

Louise had not the faintest idea of how to get to Africa. She did not know what happened to missionaries—especially women missionaries. She couldn't remember ever seeing one return home when he or she got old. She supposed they were eventually eaten by cannibals. She knew her eyes were bad. If she went to Africa, there would be no doctors to help her. She would probably go blind from neglect.

With effort, she pushed Satan's grim picture from her.

"Well, Lord, if I can find a way, I'm going to go to Africa. I'll be a little old woman sitting on a box in front of a mud hut. I'll be stew in a cannibal pot. But if You don't tell me You don't want me, I'm going to Africa."

The room lit up as though it were on fire. Louise leaped to her feet. Her heart felt like a feather. Weeping with joy, she thought, I'll not tell anyone about this. I'll wait and see what God does.

Then she rushed from the room and told everyone she met.

Within a few weeks, Louise shared in a revival with another woman evangelist. Florence went with her. They began the service with a prayer meeting. Five people came. As they prayed, the burden for meetings became intense. Louise lay in the straw, unconscious of the others. God told her to fast and pray until revival came. She later told this to the others and learned God had spoken to each of them in the same way. They began to fast and pray in earnest. Hours were spent in prayer.

The first night, the service was cold and prayerless. The second night, God helped them preach.

At midweek, revival came. The whole congregation came to the altar. That day, Louise took a piece of bread and a dill pickle for food. She and Florence continued to pray and fast the rest of the week.

Though Louise had promised God she would preach "until He told her to quit," preaching did not come easy. In the summer, she went out with another woman to hold a revival at Halfway, Oreg. The first night, a neighboring preacher came to the service. Louise was scared of this experienced man of God. She stumbled and faltered in her message. At the end, she fled out the back door to her room. "I told You I couldn't preach!" she sobbed. "I'm not going to preach again until I learn how."

The next morning, she met a woman who had been at the service. The woman thanked her for her message. "God used it to bring me to victory," the woman said.

Louise took courage and dared to try again.

Sometimes, as she preached holiness, Satan would come with doubts.

"Are you sanctified yourself?" he would taunt. "When?"

Desperately, Louise prayed, "Lord, You did such a good job in saving me, I never could doubt it. When You called me to Africa, it was the same way. No one could make me doubt that. But if I am going to preach holiness, why didn't You do a better job of giving me that experience? I have sought it many times. I need to know."

God said, "What did I do for you that day in your room?"

"Called me to Africa."

"Did you ever before turn everything over to Me?"

"No, Lord, but I'm still afraid of people. I'm bound."

Then God showed Louise a narrow coffin. She was in it. It had no lid. She could get out if she chose.

"You are free," God said. "But use not freedom as an occasion to the flesh."

Now Louise understood. When the burden fell off in that room on the day she had said yes to God's call to Africa, God had sanctified her. She felt ready to fly. Now she could preach holiness, not just because she believed in it, but because she knew the Holy Spirit had indeed cleansed her heart.

In December 1917, as Louise was in her room reading her Bible, she was nearly overcome with a heartbreaking burden for someone she did not know. She saw the figure of a young man in khaki-colored clothes. He was in some kind of terrible danger. She cried and prayed for hours.

Louise prayed through the night. Early the next morning, she saw God put a robe on the man and a ring on his finger. God handed Louise a scroll of pardon. Then he turned the figure around. It was her brother, Frank, who was not a Christian. She praised God for this assurance of Frank's salvation and continued to claim it for 40 years, as Frank resisted the appeal of the Holy Spirit.

Forty years later, Frank walked into a service where Louise was preaching and yielded his life to Christ. He had two years of joyous walking with Christ before God took him home.

During the summer of her junior year in college, a group of the students went up the Lewis River fishing and camping. The group was so noisy, Louise went on ahead to fish in quiet. She knew there was a rock ledge jutting into the river there. When she reached it, she crawled over the ledge to where a 15-foot waterfall dropped into a deep pool. Casting her line into the pool, she caught several big trout. Suddenly, she became aware that she was sliding slowly toward the edge of the fall. She threw her basket and pole toward the bank to free her hands. The motion sent her plunging over the edge into the pool below. She was battered against the rocks on one side and then into the middle. She grabbed for the protruding rocks and held on grimly. She thought she was going to die. But God said, "No, you won't die. Hang on."

She caught hold of a craggy rock and found a foothold, braced herself against the rocks behind her and held on desperately, with the water swirling swiftly just under her chin. She shouted, hoping someone would hear and come to help.

The boys were working their way up the river. Louise heard them laughing and talking. She shouted again.

One of the boys said, "That's Louise, and her voice is coming from where it shouldn't be."

Louise saw her brother, another boy, and Florence come into view.

They stood on the ledge, their faces as white as chalk. She began to laugh.

"Don't laugh," her brother shouted. "You're about to drown."

The boy with them knew the river well. He said he would go up the river and come down on the same rock as Louise, and try to get to her. In a few moments, she heard him on the other side of the rock.

"Can you work yourself around toward me?" he called.

Louise felt for footing and slowly edged her way around to his side. Together they crawled up on top of the rock. Other boys came and formed a human chain and got them out of the racing water and back to safety on the ledge.

The following year, President Wiley addressed the students in chapel. Soberly, he urged the students to do something to help the college. "We are in deep need of revival," he said. "Take this need on your hearts and pray. God must help us."

His urgency captured the students' hearts. Moved by the Holy Spirit, a woman offered her home to any who wanted to come and pray.

Seven students gathered at her home, determined to pray all night and attend classes by day until revival came. For seven nights they came and wept and pleaded with God to send revival. On the seventh night, sometime after midnight, Louise rose from her knees exhausted, and started to go home to bed. She had scarcely left the room when she heard the familiar Voice, "Louise, what doest thou here?"

She ran back to the prayer room. "God's beginning to talk," she cried.

The students clapped their hands and began to praise God for the revival He was going to send.

They went to the college. People were screaming and crying out in prayer. No one went to breakfast. Someone brought the cook to the chapel to join them in prayer. Classes all turned into prayer meetings. Disagreements were settled, wrongs straightened out. Students exhorted. There was no preacher. God moved through the whole town, reviving churches and cleaning up lives. Scores were sanctified before the revival subsided.

It was an exhilarating experience. Now Louise had seen what God could do when even a small group of His children were willing to fast and pray in desperate earnestness for revival.

3

To Africa

In June 1920 Louise graduated from Northwest Nazarene College. She had completed one more step in God's training, and He was ready to lead her on to larger adventures.

She applied for missionary appointment and sailed for Africa in October 1922.

On board the ship, Louise met an older missionary couple returning for a term of service. Privately, she thought they looked dowdy and grim, and she made no effort to seek their company. She cheerfully visited with the ship's captain and crew and the other passengers. Her actions were duly noted and reported to the mission leaders when the couple arrived in Africa.

Louise arrived in Africa as green and ignorant as any missionary had ever been. But she came determined to learn and to be as good a missionary as she could with God's help.

Many of Louise's experiences as a missionary in Africa are told in her book *Africa, O Africa.*

God never let success come easily or effortlessly.

Louise spent four years at Sabie learning the Zulu language. Each day, she went out and sat with the African women in their homes, practicing Zulu, and listening to their corrections. As she practiced, she was also learning firsthand the customs and concerns of the people of Africa—an invaluable lesson.

A few months after arriving, she visited a demon-possessed woman with some of the mission boys. The woman screamed and spit at them. When Louise prayed, the woman dropped down as though dead. But when Louise stopped praying, the woman leaped up again, roaring defiance. Louise did not know how to deal with demons. She sent one of the boys to call the church together to pray. Suddenly the woman screamed, "We're coming! We're coming!"

Three non-Christian women sitting in the hut leaped up and rubbed ashes on the woman's head. She began to laugh.

"We won't come out now," she chortled. "Those three won't let us out."

The sense of God's presence left the house. Baffled, Louise returned to her home.

After her years of language study, Louise went to a council meeting, hoping to learn of a permanent assignment. General Superintendent Hiram F. Reynolds talked with her, asking searching questions. Then he said, "I came here expecting to have to send you home. I didn't know you were devoted to missions body and soul."

It was quite some time before Louise learned that the report of the older missionaries who had been on the boat had come close to causing her to be dismissed from missionary service.

When assignments were made, Louise was put in charge of the girls at Endingeni. She had not been there long before she discovered that the missionaries were subsisting on the common African food of maize, pumpkin, and greens, with occasionally a little meat.

"Don't you plant gardens?" she asked in amazement.

"We've tried. Nothing will grow here but corn and pumpkins," they replied.

Louise looked at the lush pumpkin vines, the tall corn. If those will grow, other things will grow, she decided. She asked questions of the Swazis, learned the time for planting in Swaziland, and began to introduce onions, lettuce, cabbage, carrots, tomatoes, and squash. Planted at the right time, they grew well. Soon she was providing work for school students and food for everyone on the station.

Pleased with the vegetable gardens, Louise began to plant fruit trees: bananas, oranges, tangerines, grapefruit, pecans, apples, papaws, plums, and guavas soon were a regular part of mission food.

The hard lessons Louise had learned in college now brought dividends. She knew that God did not do for people what they could do for themselves. He guided and encouraged, but the sweat and tears came from the people.

She learned to work like 10 men. The Swazi girls were not used to the stress of constant work needed to keep the mission functioning. When God showed Louise a vision of the Endingeni mission hillside covered with brick buildings, she knew she had to inspire the students to help her bring the vision to reality. She soon discovered that the girls and women worked willingly if she was working with them. Daily, she dug to level the hillside, then mixed clay and sand and cement for bricks. Side by side, muddy and weary, she cheered and urged, and moved to the rhythm of the older women who sat on the bank singing to cheer them on. And the buildings were built, one at a time, with a God-sent bricklayer who appeared each season at the exact time they needed him and left when the job was done.

There were times when the driving energy of the young missionary from the northwest chafed under the placid easy-going tempo of Africa. Sometimes, her drive to move ahead brought her into more trouble than she anticipated.

On one occasion, she was returning from a meeting with a group of the Swazi boys and girls. The girls strolled along, enjoying their holiday from school and gardens. The boys moved at a faster pace and soon outdistanced them. Louise, on her mule, Coffee, grew tired of trying to stay back with the slow-moving girls.

"You girls come along," she admonished. "I'm going to ride ahead and catch up with the boys."

She urged her mule into a gallup on the trail, expecting to join the boys very soon. She reached a very lonely place where the trail crossed a river. There was no sight or sound of the boys.

As Louise approached the river, she saw, on the other side, the feet of two men standing in the water. They were concealed in the thick bushes. She knew they had seen her, and that they knew she had to cross at that spot. Not willing to let them know she was fearful, she plunged in and urged the mule across. At the opposite bank, one man leaped out with a big club raised over his head.

"Look out!" Louise yelled. "This mule is wild. He'll kick if you get too close." She jogged the mule on the off side, causing him to jerk and twist in the river. The two men dodged his flying hooves.

Louise recognized one of the men as the father of a little boy she had cared for when he was ill. The other was his apprentice. She knew their work—they were assassins for the witch doctor in the area.

"What are you grown men doing down here in the river in the middle of the day?" she chided. "Why aren't you weeding in the gardens instead of leaving it for the women to do?"

She turned to the older man and asked him how his little boy was doing. Then she urged him to keep the young man with the club away from the restive mule lest he be injured.

After a long delay, the older man told the youth to move back and put down his club.

When the path was clear, Louise urged her mule slowly ahead, talking to the men all the while, until she was out of the river. Then she gave the mule a sharp slap with her whip and sent him galloping across the plain toward the mountain. She climbed the lower slopes at a fast trot, hoping to beat the men if they should try to run around the mountain and intercept her on the other side. Anxious hours later, Louise reached the mission safely.

Harrowing as it was, the experience faded from Louise's memory in the pressure of busy days.

There came another day when Louise was returning from a meeting with a group of the school boys and girls. They had arranged for the boys to leave at dawn. The girls were going to follow later with the supplies they had brought to the meeting.

Again, the girls moved slowly along the trail, stopping to rest when their loads became too heavy. Louise was eager to get back to the mission. At midmorning she said to the girls, "I'm going on ahead and catch up with the others. Come on as fast as you can. You don't want to be out in the bush after dark."

Louise was not aware that the boys had risen at midnight in order to travel while it was cooler. They were hours ahead of her.

Louise rode off at a gallop, then slowed to a brisk trot, listening for voices on the trail ahead. At midday, she stopped to feed the mule and eat her lunch. She loosened the saddle girth to let the mule feed in comfort.

As she sat on a log eating, she saw an African man coming up the trail. He was obviously drunk. She recognized him and knew that in his drunken state he could be very dangerous.

"What are you doing here alone?" he asked, stopping beside her.

She stood up, "I'm not alone," she said, moving toward the mule. "I have friends just ahead on the trail, and others are just back there a little way, coming."

But the man knew he had just walked on that trail and there were no others close by. He moved toward her.

Louise edged around the mule, trying to tighten the saddle girth. The man followed her. She dodged from side to side, keeping the mule between them.

"Watch out!" she warned. "This mule will kick if you get too close." At last she got the girth tightened. She picked up her lunch sack.

"Do you like bread?" she asked, holding it out to the man. "Here is some especially good bread and some fruit."

True to custom, the man accepted the sack with both hands and peered into it. Louise leaped into the saddle, pulled the reins tight, and kicked the mule. The man lunged for her, barely missing her as the mule leaped ahead on the trail. She kept up a brisk trot most of the way home.

It was a year or more later that Louise was coming home with a group of the young people from a meeting in the lowveldt. The young people started off briskly, while Louise remained behind talking with the adults. As the men and women left, Louise started up the trail to catch up with her group, already far out of sight. Somewhere along the way, Louise took a wrong turn. She rode for hours, getting more lost with every branch in the trail. She had no idea where she was. Everything looked strange. The sun sank low in the sky. Louise prayed urgently for God to send someone to guide her.

In a few moments, she heard the clip-clop of hooves. Around the bend came a man on a mule.

Louise recognized him. It was reported that he was the witch doctor's assassin.

The man knew her also. "Greetings," he said. "Aren't you the girl at Umfundisi Schmelzenbach's? What are you doing way down here?"

Louise greeted him politely. "I'm glad you came along. I prayed and asked God to send help and you have come. I'm lost. I don't know where I am."

The man named the low dip in the trail where they had met. It was miles down in the lowveldt in the opposite direction from where she wanted to be. He pointed to a mountain in the distance. "See? That is where you should be."

"Will you guide me back to where I will know the way?" Louise asked.

The man grunted. "I'm tired," he protested. "I've been all day at the witch doctor's. I don't want to go the long distance back."

Louise pleaded with him to guide her at least part way.

Reluctantly, he rode ahead of her back along the trail for five miles or more. "Now," he said, pointing ahead toward the landmark, "keep your eyes on that mountain. When you go down into a dip and can't see the mountain, pick up a landmark that lines up with it, and follow that until you can see the mountain again." He wheeled his mule around and retraced his way.

Louise rode on alone in the rapidly increasing darkness. Even at night, the mountain was a clear landmark against the sky. She reached the mission at daybreak.

This time, she had learned her lesson.

"Lord, thank You for bringing me safely home," she prayed. "I promise I will never again go anywhere without a guide. And when I am with a group, I'll stay with them, no matter how slow they travel."

Africa was not all adventurous, riding over jungle trails. Louise was in Africa to win people to Christ, not for adventure.

Very early, she learned that the African people were no more eager than Americans to give up their favorite sins. Forgiveness, yes. Forgiveness was good, but to change their lives—that was a different matter. Furthermore, this was territory where Satan had ruled unimpeded for years before missionaries came. Satan did not give up his victims without a battle. Now Louise understood some of the hard lessons God had taught her as a young Christian.

Prayer was her first weapon against the enemy. Prayer was the beginning of every day. If work demanded that a person rise at daybreak, then prayer demanded that he rise before daybreak. Prayer came first, whatever else needed to be done.

There was a prayer hut at the mission. Here, students from the crowded dormitories came to pray. Sometimes the girls were assigned a time of day when the hut was theirs, and the boys were given another time. Sometimes the missionaries resorted there for praying and fasting without disturbing others. Often Louise and some of her Swazi coworkers went to the hut to pray through the night for special burdens.

From her early years in college, Louise knew that 30 brief minutes of prayer brought few results. Days of fasting and prayer preceded every spiritual breakthrough in her missionary career.

In the early years, as she supervised the Swazi girls, she often had to confront angry relatives threatening violence to regain control of the runaways. Sickness, drought, hailstorms, angry chiefs, and rebellious sinners were prayed into submission to God's will, not easily, but through agonizing, unrelenting, holding on to God. With each victory, the faith of the Swazi Christians grew stronger. A holiness church was established that knew how to pray until God answered.

It had been a long journey from the little green missionary termed "incapable" by her superiors, to this intrepid prayer warrior loved and respected by the people.

There had been great high points of victory—God's challenge to build permanent buildings on the mission hill at Endingeni with no money, no building materials, nothing but God's challenge to do it. And the ingenious way God directed her to the sand and clay and everything needed when she stepped out in blind faith to begin. The healing of a deep rift between Swazi leaders and missionaries because of misunderstanding of the language—healed through an unprecedented prayer retreat with total fasting—open only to those willing to do it.

Louise had seen sick persons healed, demons cast out, desperate cases saved and wonderfully sanctified.

It seemed as though she was at the peak of her usefulness to God as a missionary when she returned to the United States for furlough in December 1940.

4

"Not Go Back"

Early in her deputation schedule, Louise was traveling with Dr. and Mrs. A. E. Sanner to a service. As they discussed workers adjusting to new situations, God spoke so clearly it seemed the Sanners could hear Him too, "Thou remaineth . . . not go back."

Louise was startled. What could that mean? She was certain God had called her to Africa, and she knew she was needed there. Many times during the year the strange words returned, "Not go back."

They were so unreasonable she assumed they were a trick of Satan, and she refused to consider them.

She was kept busy in Women's Foreign Missionary Society Conventions and often stayed on for the assembly sessions that followed, hungry for the spiritual messages of the presiding general superintendents.

God began to suggest that he had a new assignment for her. This, too, was so improbable that she feared it was Satan trying to draw her out of God's will.

The war in Europe was increasing in furor. It appeared that the whole continent would soon be involved. Louise was eager to get back to Africa while shipping was available. Several times, she booked passage on a plane or ship only to have her space cancelled to make room for military personnel.

It looked very ominous. Could this be the meaning of the words that had haunted her all year? Was God telling her that she would not be able to return?

"Lord, if the door opens, I will go," she promised.

In November 1941 she was able to secure passage on a ship leaving from New York on December 7. She was elated and hastened her packing to get ready to leave. On December 6 her crates were safely on board ship, and she was in a hotel room in New York with two other missionaries, waiting to board ship the next morning.

They awakened on December 7 to newspapers and radios screaming the news of the bombing of Pearl Harbor. "U.S. and Japan at war!" the newsboys shouted on every street corner. Louise's first thought was, "That's in the Pacific. We can still sail."

But the telegram from Kansas City soon dashed her hopes. BOOKING CANCELLED. TRAVEL TOO DANGEROUS.

In vain, Louise tried to persuade the missions office to cancel her appointment, let her travel at her own risk, and then reinstate her when she reached Africa. They would not consider it.

While the others slept peacefully that night, Louise sat numbly in a chair, praying for direction. Late in the night, the Lord broke through her anguish, "Did I not say unto you, Go not?"

"Yes," Louise replied, "You did, but the door opened."

God said, "Now I have closed the door. I have a new assignment for you here in America. It is for the world."

Through the night they talked together. Once, God seemed to intimate that marriage might be involved. This seemed utterly preposterous to Louise. She wondered if perhaps this was not God, but Satan, trying to trick her into making a fool of herself.

Louise soon was busy again in conventions. Frequently, Dr. J. B. Chapman was the presiding general superintendent in the following assembly. Louise felt her soul fed when she could stay and listen to his messages.

At one place, the workers were invited for a meal at a layman's home. It was a hot day, and they ate in the kitchen.

Dr. Chapman took off his coat, rolled up his sleeves, and slid onto a bench with the children at one side of the table. He was quite at home and kept everyone entertained with his amusing talk.

When the meal was over, Louise went with the young daughter into the living room. They sat on the davenport and visited. Soon, the girl's mother called her to come and help with dishes. As she left the room, Dr. Chapman entered and sat down beside Louise on the sofa. Abruptly he asked, "How old are you?"

Louise looked up in surprise. "Forty-nine, why?"

"I just wanted to know," he replied. "Nearly 50, isn't it?" He got up and left the room.

What a strange man! Louise thought.

Later, when God repeated His word to her, "I have a new assignment for you, it may include marriage," the name of Dr. Chapman suddenly crossed her mind. Ridiculous! she thought. I'm sure that idea is from Satan!

Each time Dr. Chapman's name came to her mind, she resolutely blocked it out. If she saw his picture on a paper, she turned it over. When she knew he was to be the assembly speaker, she began leaving after the WFMS Convention ended.

One day when she was walking down the street in a large city, the words came to her, "Behold the man whom I spake to thee of" . . . yesterday (1 Sam. 9:17).

She looked up and found herself face-to-face with Dr. Chapman. She had not known he was even in that part of the country.

She greeted him politely, feeling confused and self-conscious. What was God trying to tell her? Or was it God at all?

Sometime later, circumstances required her to remain at the assembly following her convention. Dr. Chapman preached a masterful message on the Prince of Israel. God anointed his message, and the people were blessed.

Louise went on to Washington, D.C. With time to spare, she visited the Smithsonian Institution. Sitting on a bench under Lindbergh's plane, the *Spirit of St. Louis,* she gazed up at the fragile little craft, trying to imagine what it must have been like to start out over the ocean, alone, in such a plane. She became aware of someone behind her and turned around. There stood a magnificent golden angel with outstretched arms.

"Blessed art thou among women," he said. "Are you willing for God to have His way with you?"

Awed by the glorious creature, Louise replied submissively, "Thy handmaiden hath nothing in her house. All I have belongs to God."

Slowly the golden angel faded from sight. Louise sat stunned. What on earth could his strange words mean? I have to get these things straightened out, she decided.

She rented a room from a Nazarene friend in Washington, D.C., and prepared to fast and pray until she learned what God wanted of her. Her thoughts had been in such turmoil she had not been able to eat or sleep. It had to be settled.

Locking the door, she fell to her knees beside the bed.

"Lord, You have revealed many things to me in the past. You have always made Your will plain to me. I'm grateful for Your leadership and Your patience. If You will just once more speak to me in a voice I can understand, I promise I will no longer ask about the matter, but I will leave it to You completely to do as You please and to work everything out right for me."

She picked up her Bible and it fell open at Ezekiel 44. She read, "The gate . . . which looketh toward the east . . . was shut. Then said the Lord unto me; This gate shall be shut. It shall not be opened" (vv. 1-2). This was the answer to her question about returning to Africa.

Reading on in Ezekiel 45 she saw, "It shall be for the whole house of Israel. . . . Let it suffice you" (vv. 6, 9). Here was the answer to her question about a new assignment—it was work for the whole church.

Then she read, "And a portion shall be for the prince" (v. 7).

Her thoughts went back to the recent convention when Dr. Chapman had preached on "The Prince of Israel." As she had listened she had thought, And he is a prince himself.

"All right, Lord," she said silently. "I have my answer. I will no longer discuss with anyone whether this is or is not Your will. But I will not myself try to open any doors. You will have to make all plans and open all doors."

"Will you at least be friendly?" God replied.

"Yes, I'll be friendly," she answered.

At her next convention, Louise was at the bookstand, searching for a good book to buy. As she turned to leave, she saw Dr. Chapman seated at a little table with a pile of his books in front of him. He held out a book to her. "Let me give you one of my books," he said.

She read the title and said, "Oh, I already have a copy of this," and handed it back.

She turned away and God said, "I thought you promised to be friendly."

Louise turned around and said, "I have a copy of that book, but I don't have this one," and picked up one of Dr. Chapman's other books on the table.

"Give your copy to a friend and take this one," he said, holding out his book again. "I've autographed this one for you."

Later, at the Colorado Camp, Louise was preparing for a service as the missionary speaker. God came to her in unusual anointing. She thought He was trying to give her a message to preach. She read from Prov. 22:19-21, "That thy trust may be in the Lord, I have made known to thee this day, even to thee. Have not I written to thee excellent things in counsels and knowledge, that I might make thee know . . . that thou mightest answer the words of truth to them that send unto thee?"

At that moment there was a knock at the door. A friend handed Louise three letters in the same handwriting. They were from Dr. Chapman. Every day after that came another letter in which he wrote about places where people could get married. In one letter he said, "I have to go to Mexico in the fall. That would be a great place for a honeymoon."

In one letter, he said, "We are both free and over 18. We can make our own decisions. Since we both could go through Omaha to our next appointments, why don't we meet there and have breakfast together?"

It sounded like a good idea to Louise. It would give them a chance to talk and get better acquainted.

When Louise arrived in Omaha, Dr. Chapman met her at the train with a marriage license in his pocket. Neither of them wanted a public wedding, and both knew this was God's plan for their lives. On June 20, 1942, they were married in the Omaha, Nebr., Nazarene parsonage by Rev. H. J. Beaver. A church member brought a bouquet of field flowers for Louise to carry.

"Do you mind if I send out a few announcements?" Dr. Chapman asked.

"No," Louise answered. "That's all right, if you want to."

Then they parted. Louise went on to the Northwest to keep her appointment; Dr. Chapman to go to the East for his.

When they had finished, they returned to the Midwest and began life together.

Louise had prayed fervently that God would enable her to shift from being the energetic mission director, preacher, and teacher of Swaziland, to being a supportive wife. God did just that. She slipped into the role of supporter and confidante as though she had been trained for it.

Dr. J. B. Chapman and Louise traveled together across the North American continent. Louise promoted missions in conventions while Dr. Chapman carried on his duties as general superintendent. They discovered a delightful mutual agreement both in life-style and in spiritual concerns. Both were five o'clock in the morning risers. Both liked to spend time with God at the beginning of the day. They talked, visited, prayed, debated, planned, and played together as they criss-crossed the United States in his old red Buick.

In spite of a heavy schedule, Dr. Chapman always made time to stop and see anything of interest along the way. When they could, they returned to his summer cottage in Indian Lake, Mich. There they would rest, write, and go boating on the lake. They were beautiful days of sharing, praying, and working together.

Nineteen forty-seven was an extremely busy year. Louise and Dr. Chapman drove to Pasadena, Calif., where he lectured and Louise held missionary services. They then drove back to Washington, D.C., where both were speakers in a holiness convention. From there they went to Eastern Nazarene College for lectures and down to a convention in Florida. Then back to the Washington Pacific District to their assembly, and at last to Michigan for rest and to make plans for General Assembly.

On July 28, 1947, Louise and J. B. sat talking in the little museum beside their home until late into the night. He was full of concern for the work God had placed in his hands.

As they talked, J. B. looked affectionately at Louise. "I can't believe we have known each other such a short while," he said. "It seems as though we have always been together."

The next morning, Louise laid out a clean ironed shirt and a new pair of khaki trousers for him, but he appeared at breakfast in an old ragged, faded shirt, and pants with big holes in the knees.

Knowing that Dr. S. T. Ludwig was coming to work on General Assembly plans, Louise begged him to go and change his clothes. He went, acting like a little boy who had been told he had to wash his hands before he could eat.

After a busy morning planning, Dr. Ludwig left. Louise and Dr. Chapman ate a leisurely lunch together. The doctor had ordered Dr. Chapman to rest for at least 15 minutes after lunch. That day, July 29, he was very talkative and lay down by the ironing board where Louise was working, so that he could talk while he rested.

Later that evening, as they were going to bed, he said, "Any man could make it with a girl like you to help him."

Shortly after midnight, he called out in distress. Louise jumped up and ran to him, but he had already slipped away to heaven when she reached his side.

In that terrible instant, the glow and the joy and excitement went out of her life. Stricken, she called J. B.'s son, Paul, who was visiting there at the home. He came and took charge.

Louise was devastated. All reason for living was gone. When the funeral was over and everyone had left, Louise sat down to face the future—a bleak, somber, joyless future without the man she had loved next to God himself.

5

It Is for the World

In the desolate days following the sudden death of her husband, Louise turned to the only refuge she knew—her Heavenly Father.

"What now, Lord?" she asked. "You gave me this beautiful assignment as Dr. Chapman's wife. I did not seek it. It was Your doing—the loveliest gift You ever gave me. Now You have taken him away, and I am devastated. What shall I do? I have no job. I am no longer a missionary. How shall I live?"

Gently the answer came: "My covenant that I gave at Northwest Nazarene College still stands. If you will put Me and My work first, I will take care of you. Remember My words to you when I told you not to go back to Africa? 'I have a new assignment for you—it is for the world.' Marriage was only a part."

Louise thought of the conventions and camp meetings she and Dr. Chapman had booked. How could she bear to go alone?

"Those?" she asked.

"Yes, those, first," God answered. "And afterward others as they come. I need you to share your love and burden for missions with Nazarenes in many places."

Her grieving heart cried, "But, Lord, I'm not sure I can handle going to these places alone. We had expected to serve together."

Quietly God replied, "I'll be there."

In a few weeks, Louise picked up the assignments and began to travel, alone, across America. Memories flooded over her at every step. There were many tears shed in the privacy of motel rooms. She pushed doggedly on, eventually moving into new assignments and her own ministry away from the painful memories.

Rumors began to come to her that her name was going to be nominated for the president of the Women's Foreign Missionary Society in June 1948, when Susan Fitkin retired.

She was aghast. "Oh, no, Lord," she cried. "Don't let them make that mistake. I'm not qualified. I know nothing about the work they do here at home."

God replied, "You don't need to know. I'll give you helpers."

She recalled a visit she had made to the General Council when she was a missionary. Three of the group were elderly ladies with ear trumpets, to whom everything had to be shouted. This can't be what God wants for me, she thought. "Lord, don't let them make this mistake."

General Convention came. Louise Chapman was elected general president of WFMS.

"Lord, how will I live?" Louise asked. "This position pays no salary. I travel all the time now and barely cover my expenses."

"This is the rest of My assignment for you," God answered. "This is for the world. And My covenant still stands. Trust Me."

Louise was soon gripped by the need to make Nazarene women aware of the great prayer and financial needs of missions. Prayer and Fasting was promoted with enthusiasm, urging parents to include the children and make the meal a time of fasting for adults, of eating simple food like soup or cereal for the children, each child given his own quarter to put in his personal Prayer and Fasting envelope. She urged parents to tell a missionary story, talk about missionaries, and pray with the children for specific requests. The challenge caught on, and the Prayer and Fasting offering increased dramatically.

Along with the world needs, Louise carried a private concern of her own. From the time that Indian Lake had become her home, she had been concerned because there was no Nazarene church in Indian Lake. Retired persons were coming there to live in increasing numbers. Young families were spending their summers there. The local community of Vicksburg was growing. Yet, except for district assembly and an annual camp meeting, there was no Sunday School and no church in which to worship on Sundays. She and Dr. Chapman had talked about it but were away too much to do anything about it. Now she began to talk about it among the Nazarene families who spent summers and winters there.

Her interest was shared by several. They began to pray and plan and look around for a possible location. A group began to meet, praying and sometimes fasting to find a way to build a church debt-free.

One night, Grandma Ward was so blessed she shouted her praise to God and laughed with holy delight. The group shared her laughter and praise. When they disbanded to go home, they found the neighbors gathered outside ready to call the police.

Instead of being embarrassed, the Nazarenes excitedly told the neighbors about their plans to build a church. The community people were not quite sure what kind of church this was going to be, but eventually many of them began to support the plan.

Louise plunged into the campaign as though she were building the mission on the hill at Endzingeni. She challenged everyone to trust God and pledge beyond what they thought they could pay. One little retired woman who lived in a tiny trailer house gave the $500 she had saved for her burial expenses. A local farmer and his wife provided most of the money to pay for the lot on which to build. Everyone donated time and energy to help. Rev. Van Wuffin and the men worked almost all night finishing the inside of the small, prefabricated chapel. Lois Silvernail and Louise laid the slabs of sticky asbestos insulation that were put in the top of the church and diligently screwed the pews into position on the floor.

When the church was finished, Mr. Gilow became its loving janitor. Every Sunday, neighbors brought beautiful flowers for the sanctuary. The mothers of the church raised the funds for the Educational Budget—their share of the support for Olivet Nazarene College at Kankakee, Ill.

Children of the church placed two one-gallon bottles on the altar and led the church in giving to raise its full share of district and general budgets. The Chapman Memorial Church of the Nazarene was organized in 1950.

There were some difficult years in the life of the church. Years when Louise prayed and fasted and gave beyond her ability to keep the church alive. She saw Chapman Memorial become a strong, thriving church of 350 members, with dreams of expansion.

Louise challenged the church to build a fellowship hall and kitchen. She frequently reminded them of Dr. Chapman's favorite story, "Raise Your Own Kittens."

It was the story of an old flour miller who said he had learned that, if he wanted cats that would stay in the mill and catch mice, he must raise his own kittens in the mill. Then it became their home and they did not wander away.

"If we want holiness leaders for our church tomorrow," Louise challenged, "we must raise them in the church today. Make room for them. Nurture them. Introduce them to holiness early in life." While promoting the establishment of Chapman Memorial Church, Louise did not lessen her activity for the WFMS. She knew that in the 1920s, when the General Budget was first introduced, there had been unhappiness on the part of some who were used to giving only to the departments of the church that held their interest. She felt that the WFMS must provide one avenue through which people could give and know that their gifts would go entirely to foreign missions. For years, Prayer and Fasting became that avenue. Then the general leaders decided the needs were so critical they must put Prayer and Fasting giving into the General Budget. It was a serious disappointment to Louise and the General Council. They had always promoted and supported the Easter and Thanksgiving offerings, but Prayer and Fasting had been their special channel for foreign mission giving. They had recently discontinued their Life Membership Plan, which seemed to have passed its peak of usefulness. With the loss of the Prayer and Fasting channel, they were left with no avenue through which to give specifically for foreign missions.

The WFMS Council meeting that year was an animated time of discussion.

"We must support the full program of the church," Louise urged. "We must continue to support General Budget. But let's pray for God to give us some avenue through which we can give something extra that will go 100 percent to foreign missions. We are the Foreign Missions Department's arm in the local churches, just as the departments of Sunday School and Nazarene Young People's Societies have their local groups in the churches. Missions is our only emphasis. Missions is our reason for existence."

The council came to no decision that year and were urged to pray and try to bring a workable suggestion to their next session.

Elizabeth Vennum, a council member, was ill with the flu when she left Kansas City for her home. As she lay in her berth on the train, she was challenged by the story of the woman who brought her alabaster jar of expensive perfume, broke the seal, and poured the contents on Jesus' feet.

A love gift, Elizabeth thought. That's what we need. Not another sacrifice offering like Prayer and Fasting, but a love gift—an over-and-above gift.

Thoughtfully she drew up the plan for the Alabaster Offering. It was to be a gift of love—perfume money, she called it, like the woman had given to Jesus. Challenge people to go without something they want but don't really need and give the price to Christ as a love gift.

The completed plan presented in 1949 designated the funds to be used only for buildings on Nazarene mission fields. Alabaster offering boxes were designed and given out, sealed against opening. People were challenged to put their gifts in the boxes through the year and bring the boxes in February and September. The seals would be broken and the gifts poured out as a love gift to Christ. No one would know what anyone else gave. There would be no set goal per person.

The plan was met with the enthusiasm by the church in North America and across the world. The poorest person could gather a few coins in a box and pour them out for Jesus with the others.

Alabaster Fund giving grew rapidly. Mission fields began to take on a new look. In place of pole-and-mud-thatched-roof churches, there appeared attractive wood, cement block, and brick buildings. Neat cement block parsonages gave pastors respect in their communities. Bible college buildings, clinics, and missionary homes were built. The needs multiplied faster than the offerings could match, but every field received some help from Alabaster offerings.

Louise realized that God had given her a special gift for raising money for Him. She accepted the gift humbly, using it to challenge weak churches, small churches, and large churches to enlarge their vision and give beyond their small concepts to advance the cause of Christ.

Following the General Assembly of 1948, the Church of the Nazarene was faced with the need to increase its giving dramatically to meet the mandates handed down by the General Assembly. So much of the General Budget was allocated to these new needs that it appeared the foreign missions program would have to be drastically reduced.

Faced with the grim possibility of bringing missionaries home and closing some fields, the Department of Foreign Missions appointed a committee to try to come up with some plan to save the missions program. An all-night prayer vigil was called. Through the dark hours, Louise Chapman and the others prayed, fasted, and wept before God. As dawn was breaking, Louise lifted her head and discovered she was on top of the table in the meeting room. On the floor, prostrate in prayer were the others. Dr. Paul Updike rolled back and forth in agonized prayer pleading with God for an answer. Out of the depths of her own concern came the words of Gen. 14:20—"And [Abram] gave [Melchizedek] tithes of all." Nazarenes believed in giving a tithe of their income to their local churches. What if each church would give a tithe of all the tithes they received each month to the General Budget? This would generate regular income for the general church and support the whole program.

Louise sat up and began to tell the others. They were enthusiastic about the idea. Within a few hours, the "Tithe of the Tithes" program, later broadened to "The 10% Program," was formulated and presented to the General Board. They adopted it and took it to the District Superintendents' Conference in 1949. The superintendents went home to challenge their churches to respond. Money began to come in. The missions program of the church was saved. No missionaries were brought home.

While Louise was traveling across the nation, challenging Nazarenes to pray and give for missions, her heart was burdened for the lost world. It seemed as though Nazarenes were making so little impact against the vast needs around them. At every General Council meeting, Louise challenged the women to reach out for more *Other Sheep* subscriptions, more Prayer and Fasting members, more readers, and more giving for missions. It was unthinkable to her to keep the same goals for more than one year.

Increasingly, Louise was troubled by the thousands of men in the church who were not being personally challenged to give and pray and work for missions. In spite of misgivings on the part of some, she suggested that men be invited to become members of the WFMS.

There were questions—would the men take over the organization that women had loved so much? Would the women be crowded out? Would the men change the purpose and goals and methods that had always seemed to work well? Admittedly, the men had more money to give. They needed to be challenged with the world needs.

In 1952 the vote passed in the General Convention to invite men to become full members of the WFMS and to change the name to the Nazarene Foreign Missionary Society. It was a triumphant day. Louise lost no time in letting the men know they were not in the society for a free ride. She stirred them to pray, to give, to read, to share in all the concerns of the NFMS.

That custom-shattering convention was scarcely over before Louise and the General Council launched a search for a fitting special effort to celebrate the 40th anniversary of the NFMS. In conference with the executive secretary of the Department of Foreign Missions, they chose to raise a great offering to open a new field—Papua New Guinea—one-half of an island in the South Pacific then under the protection of Australia. The description of people still living in the stone age, unaware that there was any more to the world than their own island, caught the imagination of Nazarenes everywhere. Offerings poured in from all over the world.

On October 15, 1955, Sidney and Wanda Knox and their small son, Geron, arrived in New Guinea and soon located a mission site in the rugged highlands area. Three years later, to the day, Sidney Knox went to heaven, a victim of cancer. By then, other missionaries were in New Guinea to carry on the work.

6

The Challenges Multiply

Louise soon realized that being president of the NFMS did not require her to spend all her time in the office in Kansas City. Indeed, she was needed far more as a roving ambassador, out among the local churches, stirring up enthusiasm and concern for missions.

Invitations to speak in conventions, assemblies, camp meetings, and local churches filled her mail. As much as possible she accepted them all, regardless of church size or promise of offering. Sometimes she did not receive enough to pay her fare to the next place, but God made it up to her somewhere else and she stayed solvent. God's covenant from Nampa days was more secure than any salary.

One of the first concerns that captured Louise's heart was the lack of Nazarene churches among the black population of the United States. A glance at statistics proved her surmise that there were literally millions of black Americans, many living in population enclaves, with only three or four tiny, struggling Nazarene churches to minister to them. The largest church, at Institute, W.Va., had only 90 members.

Trying to meet the problem, the Department of Home Missions and the general church tried to form an umbrella under which the black churches could unite for fellowship and encouragement. Scattered as they were from California to Florida and Chicago to Louisiana, it was a logistical impossibility. In 1953, a Gulf Central District was organized, encompassing most of the southern states, where the black population was heaviest. One immediate problem that surfaced was the lack of trained black holiness preachers. A Bible institute that opened at Institute, W.Va., in 1948 was having little success in attracting young black men and women to enroll.

Louise became their champion. She attended the Gulf Central assemblies, visited their churches, and challenged white churches to adopt this wide open field for evangelism.

Talking with Dr. Roy Smee of Home Missions, she learned that they were seriously considering closing the Bible institute if they couldn't pay the debt on the director's home. It seemed a tragedy.

As she sat in the West Virginia district assembly, God said, "I want you to stay after the assembly and raise the money to pay off the debt on the director's home."

It seemed an enormous undertaking. Louise told the district superintendent of West Virginia what God had said. He agreed to let her try. She asked Rev. Cunningham, director of the institute, to call a special meeting after the assembly was over and to announce that they were going to raise money to save the institute. It was a dreary, rainy night. People were anxious to get home. The crowd that stayed was small. They sat uneasily in the meeting place, wondering by what alchemy she was going to be able to accomplish what many had failed to do.

Louise stepped to the podium, read her scripture, and began to describe the vast, untouched thousands of black people in the United States needing the message of holiness and the impossibility of reaching them without trained holiness pastors familiar with their culture.

By the time she began to tell of the needs of the Bible institute, the crowd was with her. She challenged them to pledge the money to pay off the debt and establish the district and school on a sound footing. God had already told Louise what she was to pledge. She announced the figure and people looked at each other. Obviously a five-dollar bill was not going to fit here. Louise turned to Dr. Smee and Dr. John Knight, Sr. "What are you going to pledge, gentlemen?" she asked.

They responded with pledges somewhat smaller than hers, but generous.

God moved upon the service. In a spirit of hilarious freedom, the money was raised to more than pay off the debt on the home. A man who was sanctified in that service later became the pastor of a large black church in Virginia.

Louise continued to support the institute and the Gulf Central District until in the changing U.S. racial climate, segregation was outlawed, and the churches of the Gulf Central District were absorbed into the regular districts in which they were located, sharing fellowship with the longer established white churches. The Bible institute was merged with the Nazarene Bible College in Colorado Springs, offering training to those called to preach who did not have the educational credentials to enter a four-year college, or who were already college graduates and needed only Bible and theological training to prepare to preach.

At about the same time that Louise was supporting the church's ministry to black Americans, she visited the Chinese Church of the Nazarene in Los Angeles. She found them meeting in a large house spilling over with swarms of Chinese children and youth, with a smaller group of adults. The possibilities were limitless. What they needed was a church to attract more adults.

When Louise learned that Los Angeles First Church had promised to match dollar for dollar of everything they raised to build their own church, she was excited.

She preached a stirring message and challenged the Chinese congregations to raise $10,000.

Captured by Louise's enthusiasm, the people responded —adults, children, and young people. One Chinese man gave $1,000.

They raised the $10,000.

When Los Angeles First Church learned what they now owed on their promise to the Chinese church, it was their turn to be astounded. But they came through with the money, and the new church was built for the First Chinese Church of the Nazarene.

Grace Church of the Nazarene in Los Angeles, a black congregation, was struggling to survive. Rev. Roger Bowman was their newly appointed pastor. He had come to a discouraged congregation that had no vision. Roger met with Louise Chapman in a trash-filled room inside the drab, dingy church building. As Roger reported few people attending, no money, little interest, it did indeed sound hopeless. "I don't know where to begin," he ended his story.

Louise talked about the potential, the thousands of black families living in the community, the wonderful message of holiness, the power of God waiting to be harnessed.

"Go for it!" she challenged. "Begin with this building. Clean it up. Ask your most faithful folks to pitch in and help. Take an offering for some paint and fix up the rooms. Make it look neat and clean inside and out. Then invite the people to come."

She challenged Roger with stories of how God had helped them in Africa; in Institute, W.Va.; in Vicksburg, Mich.

"God's ready!" she ended. "He has the resources. Believe Him!"

People became excited as the challenge was presented. Hope soared. Everyone pledged something, even the children, to help the church get on its feet.

The church sprang to life. The people bought paint and cleaned and spruced up the sanctuary and classrooms. They were proud to invite their friends to their church. And it began to grow.

Very early in her ministry in the United States, Louise began to ask God to direct her to one special person in each meeting—someone He wanted her to adopt and nurture.

One of the first to whom God directed Louise was Lillian Della Santo, a small French woman, wife of a saloon keeper, a semi-invalid asthma sufferer. She lived in Beverly, Mass. Her neighbor was a Nazarene, who always stopped to greet Lillian when she came from church. One day she gave Lillian a copy of the Nazarene paper, the *Standard.* On the front was a picture of Dr. J. B. Chapman. Beside his picture were the words, "Be still and know that I am God." As Lillian read the words, a shiver swept over her. She knew they were from the Bible—the first words from the Bible she had ever read. She put down the paper, frightened. This was God speaking to her.

A few days later, her neighbor brought Lillian a little book. She opened it reverently, placed it in Lillian's hands, and told her to read.

Lillian looked at the pages. In astonishment, she read that Jesus loved her. Tears spilled down as the truth engulfed her. The neighbor invited Lillian to attend church with her, and Lillian accepted. That morning, the preacher announced that Mrs. J. B. Chapman was coming to speak on Wednesday night. Lillian was intrigued. A woman speaker in the church? And the wife of the great man whose picture she had seen beside the Bible verse on the *Standard.* She was eager to attend.

While Louise sat on the platform that Wednesday night, God drew her attention to the little French woman who sat near the front.

"There is your adopted spiritual child," He said.

Lillian's spiritual interest and hunger were evident. Louise prayed for her, and asked about her circumstances.

On the last evening, people were testifying. Lillian stood up. Her heart was full. She didn't know how to express what she was feeling. "If Mrs. Chapman will come to talk, I'll come every night to hear her," she said, and sat down.

The service closed. People crowded around Mrs. Chapman to talk to her. Lillian slipped out of the church and walked home alone. Her mind was full of all she had seen and heard and felt.

In Louise's mind "adopted" children are not just to be prayed for. They are to be nurtured, encouraged, loved. Louise obtained Lillian's address. In a few weeks, Lillian received an encouraging letter from Louise and a box of books about God and the Christian life. She was awed that such a great lady would pay any attention to her. She read the books, wrote, asking questions, and for 40 years that correspondence has continued. Writing about the year of "probation" the local church board asked Lillian to serve before becoming a member, Lillian said, "I knew what the members of the board didn't know—that I fell in love with Jesus."

When Lillian's husband forbade her to talk about Jesus, he found himself staring at scripture verses on mirrors, cupboard doors, desks, dinner plates, and every imaginable spot where he might put his hand.

Now 90 years old, Lillian wrote recently, "I was 48 when I first visited the Church of the Nazarene, and my God has gotten bigger and bigger and lifted up and His train fills the Temple." Encouraged by Louise, this adopted child has seen her husband, son, and granddaughter become followers of her Christ. There have been many others adopted by Louise in her years of ministry. Some for short periods, others for life. A college student, asking prayer for his finances, received a letter of encouragement and a small check.

A child wrote, confiding her concern for her parents who were having problems and asking Louise to pray.

A 10-year-old boy, answering God's call to preach in one of Louise's services, opened his eyes to find Louise kneeling in front of him. She told him God had told her that he would be a missionary in Africa one day. Then, seeing the wide-eyed astonishment of the lad, she added, "But don't worry about that now. Just be a good boy and mind God and He will lead you." The boy told his parents, and then, in boy fashion, forgot about the incident as he went on through high school, college, and seminary. At the annual meeting of the Department of World Mission and the General Board, he was appointed to Ciskei. When he called his parents to tell them about his assignment and that Ciskei was in South Africa, his mother reminded him of Louise's words 20 years before. He wrote to Louise, saying, "I don't suppose you remember that little 10-year-old boy at your altar . . . I wanted to tell you we were just assigned to Ciskei." Quickly the word came back, "Oh yes, I remember that boy very well. I have prayed for him every day since that night."

A young missionary in preparation invited Louise to dinner, hoping Louise could tell her a way to bypass the years in seminary and get a missionary assignment sooner. Instead, Louise probed the depth of her hostess's spiritual commitment and call, then urged her to prepare herself spiritually and continue her seminary studies, trusting God to place her where He wanted her at the right time. That dinner was the beginning of many years of counsel, prayer, and encouragement for Frances Vine.

And others. Countless others. It has been a personal ministry, within Louise's public ministry to the church.

Sometimes God's adoption candidates were not persons, but churches. On one occasion, Louise became deeply burdened for four Spanish congregations in Mexico that needed church buildings. The amounts were not large; a little group south of Ensenada needed $1,500; another in Ensenada needed $8,000; Agua Caliente needed $3,000; and Tijuana the larger amount of $11,000. One or two she might have dared to try to supply herself, but together they amounted to $23,000, and they needed the buildings now. It was more than she could provide. Praying earnestly for God to provide the funds, Louise waxed eloquent about the devil having all the money he needed for his work and surely God could provide for these. She was interrupted by God's voice saying, "If you feel so bad about the devil having all the money, why don't you do something about it?"

Startled, Louise replied, "How, Lord? I don't have that kind of money."

And God said, "Don't you think you and I can do it?" Louise's mind flashed back to the many times when God had, indeed, done it.

"Sure, Lord," she replied. "I believe if You want to do it, we can." She rose from her knees, convinced that God was going to take care of the four congregations.

Soon after her conversation with God, Louise was at the Preachers' Meeting in Northern California. While they sat on the platform, Dr. Roy Smee, the district superintendent, suddenly turned to Louise and said, "We are a missionary-minded people, and we haven't heard one word about missions. Louise, give us the hottest word you have on missions."

Louise stood and poured out her burden for the four Spanish congregations so desperately in need of church buildings. She told them what God had said to her. Before she could finish, a man jumped up waving a $500 check. Someone else gave $500. Others began to wave money and checks. Dr. Smee put out benches with big baskets on them. People began running up and down the aisles, shouting and laughing and dropping their money in the baskets. Twelve thousand dollars in cash was dropped into the baskets that day, and over $20,000 was pledged.

Building committees were formed of pastors who bought materials to build all the churches within a week. When Louise was invited to come to the dedication of the Ensenada church, instead of the pile of stones and dust, she saw a big white church, surrounded by a neat iron fence with grass and calla lilies in front.

On another occasion, Louise was sick in bed when God told her to get up and go to the little El Monte, Calif., church and tell them the story of how God had helped in

Mexico. The El Monte church was having financial difficulties. They had not paid their budgets for some time. People were discouraged. Louise knew they were in a meeting. She dressed and went to the church. The pastor saw her come in and greeted her. Then he walked back and said, "Would you take the service?" It was a missionary meeting. The local NFMS had prepared a program. Louise said, "No, tell them to go ahead with the program, I'll just say a little word at the end."

At the close of their program, Louise stood up and told the story of the four Spanish churches and God's word to her: "Don't you think you and I can do it?"

She related how the preachers had responded to the challenge. She ended with the challenge to the people, with God, to raise the money to pay their budgets and go to district assembly with budgets paid in full.

Excitement swept the congregation. They were not doing this alone—it was God and them in it together. Someone gave $1,000. Several gave $500. A dozen or more gave $100 each, and by the end of the service, the budgets were all paid in a spirit of hilarious enthusiasm.

7

Assignment to the World

Representing the world of missions, Louise felt she needed to know firsthand how God was working in places other than Africa. She talked it over with Him and promised that if He would open the doors and help her secure the means, she would go wherever He led and minister as He directed.

When the invitation came to visit Barbados, she accepted. She was to tour the district, preach in local churches, and stir interest in Nazarene missions and the NFMS. She made her plans to arrive on September 24, 1952.

The missionaries, Rev. and Mrs. James Jones and Rev. and Mrs. Larry Faul, planned to welcome Louise with a district quarterly meeting on her first Sunday. Quarterly meetings in Barbados were outstanding events. Nazarenes came from all across the island in taxis, buses, and bicycles. The day usually began with a baptismal and worship service, then dinner on the grounds and another service in the afternoon, all of them filled with enthusiastic singing and shouting.

Early on September 22, the island was alerted to prepare for Hurricane Janet, which was headed their way. Fortunately, the worst part of the hurricane hit Barbados at low tide, avoiding the devastation of a tidal wave. But gale winds and torrential rain ravaged the island for three hours. When the storm finally moved on across the Caribbean, the missionaries went out to assess the damage. The news was dismal. Thirty-five people had died. More than 8,000 homes were destroyed or uninhabitable. Twenty thousand Barbadians were homeless. Trees were uprooted, roads were blocked with debris, and electric lines were down.

Nine Churches of the Nazarene were flattened; nine more severely damaged. Four hundred feet of the wall around the tabernacle building site were flattened. Many Nazarenes had lost their homes—their possessions blown out to sea.

Into the midst of this devastation, Louise arrived. The quarterly meeting was held in the Hall's Road Church, which was relatively undamaged. Instead of the thousand Nazarenes who usually came, only about 500 were able to make it through the blocked streets.

The day began with a great praise service, singing as Barbadians love to sing, with tambourines and clapping.

Louise preached on, "If you don't like it, change it," telling of her experience in Africa, when God had directed her to build permanent buildings with no visible finances nor building materials. The devastated Barbadian Nazarenes were encouraged.

In the afternoon service, after enthusiastic singing, Louise stepped to the pulpit and said, "The Lord has put it on my heart to take a thank offering because none of our Nazarenes were killed by Hurricane Janet."

There was stunned silence. How could these people give an offering when many were without a home to live in or clothes to wear?

"I know you don't have money today," Louise continued. "You can pledge the money and pay it by the first of the year."

This was a new experience for the Barbadian Nazarenes. They had never been challenged to give when they had nothing. Louise exhorted them to pray, believe God, and rise to the disaster that faced them. She encouraged them, telling of impossible tasks God had enabled her to accomplish when He asked it.

Then she prayed for God to bless and challenge their faith. Louise started the offering with her own pledge of $100. The two missionary couples pledged the same. The spirit of giving moved upon the people. Many of the pastors pledged money they did not have. People shouted and praised God. The six children of the missionaries asked their parents if they could pledge, and each one pledged $25.00 without knowing where they would get the money. When the pledges were totaled, $1,400 had been promised by people whose homes and livelihood had just been destroyed by Hurricane Janet. It was one of the greatest things that had ever happened in the Barbados Church of the Nazarene. They had dared to pledge with only their faith in God as security.

When Louise spoke in the Colymore Rock Church later, the pastor introduced her by saying, "Janet was a powerful lady. She swooped down and stole our hats and jackets. She breaked our dishes and tossed the roofs of our houses into the sea. But Mrs. Chapman, she stealed our money!"

On the first Sunday of the next year, all the pledges were paid. Remarkable stories were told of the way God helped many of them pay their pledges. The experiences changed their lives.

Before she left Barbados, Louise turned the first shovel of dirt for the ground-breaking for the new district tabernacle.

From Barbados, Louise traveled to Trinidad. She told the story of the devastation Janet had caused in Barbados, and how the Nazarenes had overcome Janet by taking a great thank offering. The story stirred the Trinidad Nazarenes and later those in Guyana as well. They took offerings and sent them to Barbados to help rebuild the churches.

Louise returned to the United States and told the story of the islands in an NFMS Convention. The people enthusiastically raised $5,000 and sent it to help with the reconstruction. Within a year, all the Barbadian churches were restored and four were moved to better locations.

One of Louise's visits outside the United States was to Cuba. She went with Fairy Chism, a missionary friend, to preach in a district camp meeting. They prepared for the meeting with hours of prayer and fasting. God answered with an outpouring on a morning service in which nearly the whole congregation came to the altar seeking to be filled with the Holy Spirit.

Looking down at the crowded altar, Louise prayed, "Lord, direct me to the person with the greatest need."

She was drawn to a soldier kneeling at one end. Depending on God to translate her English into his Spanish, she began to plead with God for this man. Spanish Christians joined her. They prayed for hours as the young man wept and wrestled with his need. He prayed through to clear victory and testified, saying that in his army barracks he often became furiously angry when the men teased him. He was so desperate, he had taken his gun and gone outside to kill himself. An army friend had followed him and urged him not to do it. "Go back to your missionary," the friend said. "Try again. God has power to set you free from your terrible temper." The soldier had spent the afternoon talking with Missionary Director Lyle Prescott. That morning he had been wonderfully sanctified.

Fairy Chism returned home after the camp meeting. Louise stayed in Cuba for a district tour. Flying to the Isle of Pines for a Preachers' Meeting, she saw the sun shining on a little fishing village below.

"I have much people in this place," God whispered.

"What is that little village down there?" Louise asked Lyle.

"That is Guanimar," Lyle answered. "There is no spiritual leader there, not even a local Catholic priest."

Returning from the meeting, they again flew over Guanimar and talked about the spiritual darkness there.

Again, God said to Louise, "I have much people in this place."

In the pressure and hurry of the next few days, Guanimar was forgotten.

Louise completed her tour, returned home to the States, and was touring churches in Arizona when God awakened her in the night, saying, "I have much people in that city."

She got out of bed and wrote to Lyle, asking if he had gone back to Guanimar. She was sure God was talking to her about that village. For several nights, God woke her at midnight with the same words. She wrote to Lyle Prescott again, saying, "Go and find some property on which we can build a church in Guanimar."

When Lyle received Louise's letters, he went to Guanimar. As he walked up and down the streets of the village, he felt the same burden that had troubled Louise. A woman ran after him, jeering and laughing. Children joined in the fun. Lyle stopped and greeted them in Spanish. "Would you like to have me come here and preach about Jesus?" he asked.

Startled at hearing a foreigner speak her language, the woman said, "Yes."

Lyle returned in three days, and the woman who had scoffed, now invited him to her home. She brought in her neighbors. None had been in a church for years, if ever.

As Lyle began to preach, some listened, some chatted among themselves. Children ran in and out, followed by the neighborhood dogs.

The next day, Lyle discovered that a church, long closed, was for sale. A day later, he found land available, and a house. He wrote Louise of his findings.

Within a day, Louise received a letter saying that a woman had left $1,000 to Louise in a will. She wrote back, asking that the money be sent by airmail to Lyle Prescott in Cuba.

A year later, God awakened Louise in the night with a heavy burden for Guanimar. "I don't want property only," God said. "I want souls in Guanimar."

Louise prayed all the next day for God to move in Guanimar. A day later, she received a letter from Ardee Coolidge saying he and his wife were starting Vacation Bible School in Guanimar with preaching services at night. Louise doubled her prayers.

The Holy Spirit moved upon the services. Nearly the whole town was converted. At the close of the revival, Ardee took a picture of the group and sent it to Louise. She read the names of the new converts to the church members at Chapman Memorial Church at Indian Lake. They praised God and each chose one of the converts to adopt, and they prayed faithfully for them for months.

The new Christians in Guanimar went to surrounding villages and witnessed. Groups of believers formed. When Dr. Samuel Young visited Cuba, the new believers met him, begging for preachers. The whole southern part of Cuba was evangelized through the starting of the church in Guanimar.

In 1957, Louise returned to Africa. She had been away for nearly 20 years. What would she find? Would she be able to preach in Zulu? Would they remember her?

She hoped the missionaries would allow her a few days to rest and become reoriented to the culture before speaking. But she learned they had planned a great welcoming service within hours of her arrival. She was to be the main speaker. The welcome speeches were over quickly. As the crowd waited expectantly, Louise stood, read the scripture from her Zulu Bible, and launched into a fervent message in Zulu. The Swazis were ecstatic. Missionaries who were still using interpreters were secretly ashamed and vowed to learn Zulu. Some of the old witch doctors who had known Louise years before were there. "She speaks as though she had never gone away," they said in respectful wonder.

Louise toured the much-enlarged African church. One of her visits was to the Coloured and Indian Bible College.

The principal was a first-term missionary, Philip Steigleder. He and his wife, Mary Lou, had felt keenly that the students needed a deeper work of grace to prepare them to be true holiness preachers. For weeks, the Steigleders had been praying for God to send His Holy Spirit upon the school. There had been no visible response.

Since the classroom was also the chapel, there was no altar as such. If someone wanted to pray, he picked up his chair, brought it to the front, and knelt.

Louise preached in the morning chapel, a clear, searching message on the need for heart cleansing and total surrender to God's will. At the close of her message, every student picked up his chair and carried it to the front, earnestly seeking the experience of holiness.

The Steigleders were elated. They were sure everything had been settled now.

To their surprise, after the students had testified, Louise said, "You are beginning to make progress. Now go out and find a tree alone somewhere, and pray until you really pray through and die out to yourselves and your desires completely. Pray until you have given everything you are and have fully to God." They went.

The Steigleders took Louise on a tour of the area around the school, showing her the great population of Coloured and Indian people there.

When they returned in the early evening, they found a group of students who had spent the day praying and fasting and making restitution for wrongs done. They were gathering in the cold, unheated chapel classroom for prayer. Louise and the Steigleders joined the students. For hours, Louise agonized in prayer for God to send His Holy Spirit upon these students—to baptize them with His Spirit until they would be fervent for God and holiness for the rest of their lives.

No one dared leave as long as Louise stayed on her knees in prayer. At about four o'clock in the morning, the fire of God fell on the little praying group. One after another, the students came through in shouting victory. Revival broke out and spread to all the local churches, with sweeping scenes of repentance and restitution. Hindu idols were removed from homes, demons were cast out, and believers were sanctified wholly.

Students who had been shy and diffident preached with power on city buses, commuter trains, and street corners, as well as in churches and homes.

Pastors of all races: black, Coloured, Indian, and white, gathered at the school for days of prayer.

Long after Louise returned to America, the impact of that outpouring of the Holy Spirit was spreading across South Africa. Young men in that class of 13 became strong leaders in the Church of the Nazarene for the rest of their lives. They preached holiness with conviction and power, because they had experienced the Holy Spirit at work.

There were other scenes of victory while Louise was in Africa, but none greater than God's outpouring upon the students in the Coloured and Indian Bible College.

Louise had taken to Africa two or three wristwatches given her by American Nazarenes. She looked for missionaries who might need them. On her visit to Elizabeth Cole at the Leprosy Colony, she noticed that Elizabeth did not have a watch and gave one to her. Later when she returned home, Louise received a letter from Elizabeth, thanking her for the watch. "I lay awake last night listening to my new watch ticking," Elizabeth wrote, "and I realized that I had not had a timepiece of any kind until you came. I had not missed one, because here we live by the sun."

The tour of Africa was satisfying and heartwarming. She was encouraged by the growth of the church. She was blessed to meet old pastors she had known and old prayer warriors like Alice Kumalo who had shared burdens with her at Endingeni. Louise felt fulfilled, enriched, and encouraged as she returned home.

8

A Dream Fulfilled— and Catastrophe

Louise returned from Africa driven by the urgency to get on with the harvest—so vast were the needs—so few in the harvest fields!

She urged the NFMS to set higher goals for prayer, for giving, for members. Enlisting every Nazarene—men, women, and children—became a driving passion. The complacency of comfortable Americans chafed her spirit. Why couldn't they understand that millions were dying without Christ? Where was the burden for the lost? How could people be awakened?

She was a one-woman army, crisscrossing America, trying to give her vision to people who had never seen the world beyond their own pleasant borders.

The 50th anniversary of the NFMS was approaching. What could they do that would be a fitting celebration for that day?

In the annual sessions, the General Council considered possibilities. Persistent and pressing were the repeated requests from the missionaries in New Guinea for a hospital. Located in the remote highlands, accessible only by small plane, every day the missionaries saw patients that their small clinic was not equipped to treat.

How better could the NFMS celebrate their anniversary than to provide a hospital for the field whose opening they had funded years before.

Encouraged by the general superintendents and the World Mission secretary, the council chose the New Guinea hospital as their anniversary goal. The idea captured the hearts of Nazarenes everywhere. In a dozen different ways, churches of all sizes all over the world raised their offerings for the New Guinea hospital. The money poured into Kansas City. When the offering was complete, Nazarenes had given well over $150,000 to build a first-class, modern hospital in the remote highlands of New Guinea.

In the secret corners of Louise's heart was born a desire to see the field and the hospital the NFMS had given to the church. She voiced her wish to very few besides God, and even to Him it was not a request, only an expressed desire.

Northwest Nazarene College surprised Louise by conferring upon her the honorary doctor of divinity degree in 1963. As she received the doctoral hood, her mind was filled with memories of the years she had trudged those halls in her patched dress and scruffy shoes, learning lessons of faith and trust and intercession more valuable than all the knowledge she had gained from books.

Already in 1962, Louise and God had been having conversations about retirement. Not from God's work, but from the responsibilities as NFMS president. By January 1963 she was convinced that it was God's will for her to step down. She had never felt adequate for the assignment, and it was with a bit of relief that she sensed God was releasing her from it.

With her going, an era ended in NFMS history. Susan Fitkin and Louise Chapman had aggressively led the NFMS from the original small group of local societies to a worldwide organization working tirelessly to keep missionary fervor burning in local churches. Now the general church leaders felt it was time for the presidency to be more of an honorary position like that of the NYPS president, with the work being done by the general director in Kansas City. It took a while for their concept to filter through to those who had worked under the forceful leadership of those first two presidents.

As general president emeritus, Louise was as much in demand as a convention speaker as before. Her calendar was full. Growing in her heart was the audacious dream that if God would permit it, she might now visit not only New Guinea, but other countries in the Orient as well—that vast area of the world she had never seen.

God encouraged her dream. When word became public that she was going to visit New Guinea, invitations came in from all over that part of the world. She accepted them all. It was the fulfillment of the rest of her vision from those early years when the Man of the Mountain had shown her all the countries of the world crying out for the gospel.

With growing excitement, Louise set out on her long and last overseas journey. The journey that took her to Hawaii, Australia, New Zealand, New Guinea, the Philippines, India, Hong Kong, Japan, Korea, and Taiwan.

Every country scheduled Louise heavily, determined to let as many as possible enjoy the ministry of this woman who was a legend in the world of missions. Camp meetings, conventions, revivals, and district tours were planned end to end. To each assignment Louise gave herself without reserve. In an especially difficult revival in the Philippines, she fasted and prayed for hours, pleading for God to break through at any cost. He did, and many were sanctified.

With no chance to rest between, Louise moved on from country to country.

In Korea, she rose each day to pray with the Christians at 4:30 in the morning, and often did not get to bed until after midnight. There were days when she kept going by sheer willpower, almost too exhausted to think. Not for anything would she cancel one meeting of those that had been planned for her. If this was God's program, she would fulfill it.

Her last visit was a district tour in Alaska.

She arrived back in Portland, Oreg., totally exhausted, and stopped at her sister Florence's home to rest and visit. It was too late. By evening she could not move her legs at all. She woke in the morning, totally paralyzed, except for her voice. She could not move a finger or toe. She could not even swallow. She was taken to a Portland hospital where doctors made extensive tests. Their diagnosis was grim. Somewhere along the way she had picked up a virus that caused guillain-barre syndrome. Their prognosis: permanent paralysis. But they misdiagnosed two things: the power of God, and Louise Chapman's will to recover.

Helpless in her hospital bed, tended by nurses, friends, and therapists, Louise struggled for hours each day, willing a finger—a toe, to move.

On Thanksgiving Day, 1967, three months after she was stricken, she tried to swallow once more, and felt her throat move. "I did it! I did it!" she exulted. When the doctor came by for his daily visit, she said, "I can swallow!"

The doctor shook his head and smiled. "No, I'm afraid not," he said.

"Bring me some water," Louise pleaded. "Let me show you."

A nurse brought a glass of water and put a few drops in a spoon. Louise took a sip and swallowed it.

The doctor watched incredulously. "I can't believe it!" he exclaimed. "I never thought it could happen."

Later, Louise remembered this as the best Thanksgiving Day of her life.

Months of tedious therapy continued. But now, by infinitesimal amounts, movement returned to her body. Every new motion was cause for celebration. In March 1968, six months after she was stricken, Louise was carried by ambulance and plane to her home at Casa Robles. Her sister, Josephine, and later her friend, Buena King, moved in to care for her.

There were discouraging hours when Louise wondered how this illness could glorify God or fit into His assignment for her. If it was a devious trick of Satan to derail her ministry, she was determined to thwart his purposes. God helping her, she would walk again and continue her ministry as long as God gave her breath.

Eventually, Louise did regain enough strength to go out into ministry—perhaps too soon. Her weakened leg muscles played tricks on her. In her words, she said later, "Before I learned to live a handicapped life, I fell and broke my left leg, cracked both knees, broke my ribs four or five times and my pelvis bone. It was a hard lesson to learn. I hope I've learned it."

Doctors told her that the muscles in her legs had never come back to dependable strength.

Accepting, finally, that she was not going to be able to carry on "life as usual," Louise approached God with her dilemma. "Lord, how can I fulfill Your assignment to win souls if I can't get out to reach them?" she asked.

"Who do you think is sending all the visitors to you asking for prayer and counsel?" God replied.

Louise thought back over the weeks since she had been home. It was true. People had been coming every day. She had thought they were just coming to visit. Now she realized they had indeed come for counsel, prayer, advice, encouragement. Sometimes her prayer time spread out over most of the day as she remembered each one by name.

"Well, all right, Lord," Louise acquiesced. "If this is Your plan, I accept it. Use me as You will."

9
A New Assignment—Again?

Aware now that God was using her in a new way, Louise began to view her visitors through God's eyes. She was alert to signs of distress or concern, to troubled or discouraged hearts behind what sounded like casual questions.

"Louise is my mentor, my trusted counselor, my prayer partner," wrote Frances Vine, former missionary. "She prays and keeps others praying until God answers. I thank God for allowing me to call her my friend."

Marti was born into a Christian home but rebelled as a child. She was constantly into mischief, always choosing the wrong friends in school and college. She had begun smoking cigarettes as a child of 12, and in her teens had begun to drink beer. On her own in California, she was introduced to hard liquor and drugs, and was soon addicted.

Marti met Louise Chapman in 1975 when friends asked her to take them to Casa Robles to visit Louise. Marti was uncomfortable during the visit, and on the way home remarked, "I don't think I'd want to be one of those girls in Africa she talked about. That woman is like a general."

In 1978 Marti's friend invited her to a birthday party for Louise. Marti had no intention of going. She stalled, hoping for an excuse to refuse. She had been out of work for a year, suffering a nervous breakdown from her overuse of drugs and alcohol.

After lunch on the designated day, Marti reluctantly went to her friend's home for dessert. Louise was there. After a polite interval, Marti excused herself, saying she had to go to work. As she passed Louise, Louise pulled her down and kissed her, saying, "I'll be praying for you."

Secretly, Marti was deeply moved by Louise's caring. This was a different side to the "general."

When their mutual friend had a stroke, Marti began to call Louise to tell her how their friend was progressing.

In May 1979 she spent a weekend with Louise and went to church with her. Not long after that, Louise fractured her leg. Marti visited her in the hospital each Sunday.

By then, Marti was longing to give her heart to God, but she could not stop smoking. Driving to the hospital one day, her hunger to know God was so intense that she threw her cigarettes out the window and vowed that would be the last. That day, she knelt by Louise's bed in the hospital and gave her heart to God.

Can I keep my vow not to smoke? she wondered. Always she had smoked as she drove. On the road home, she began singing choruses she remembered. She was in her house when she realized she had not even thought of a cigarette all day.

"Lord," she prayed, "if You can keep me from even thinking of smoking for a whole day, You can keep me all my life."

Drugs and alcohol were harder to break away from, but Louise would not give up on her. Many hours were spent in prayer before Marti won her freedom from both the drugs and the alcohol. But the day came when God delivered her, sanctified her, and she declared with conviction, "I'm His forever."

To a Christian woman suffering from deep depression, Louise wrote reassuringly, "Yes, God does know how to help people who are depressed . . . I have seen God do marvels for depressed Christians. I urged one to believe that God dearly loved her and wanted to help her. I suggested that she find someone in more and worse trouble than her own and try to help that person. She did this, and then found others to help. Today, she is delivered from the depression. You must remember that God, the mighty Creator, loves you. He loves you as if you were the only one in the world to love. Think of this until it warms your heart. Then begin to help someone who needs what you have to give. God wants you to be happy and fulfilled every day of your life."

Those were heady words to one feeling unloved and useless.

To parents grieving over rebellious teenage children, Louise wrote encouraging words, telling of the prayers of the missionary group at Casa Robles and then added gentle words of advice, urging them to give more time to their children, to reassure them that they were loved and special, to shower them with kindness and praise. "Overlook her faults," she wrote to one, "until she gets past this stage. Let her see Jesus in your actions and hear Him speaking in your speech to her."

A young pastor and his wife met Louise Chapman in 1988 while visiting friends. The friends took them to Louise's home to meet Buena King. Louise came into the room about an hour after they arrived.

She asked the young preacher and his wife a few questions and he opened up, sharing his burden for souls, and the need for Christians to pray through on concerns; to fast and pray often.

Louise listened quietly, then said, "I like you and what I hear you saying. Just remember, God doesn't expect you to damage your body through excessive fasting. Let Him lead you."

Before they left, Louise stood, linked arms with the pastor and his wife, and prayed earnestly for them and their ministry. The presence and power of God filled the room.

The young pastor returned home, awed by this older woman, so intimate with God, who seemed genuinely interested in him and his wife.

A few weeks later, Louise wrote to him, sharing various ways of fasting that would not be harmful physically. At the end of her letter she added, "God has led me to add you to my prayer list. I will pray each day for you and your wife."

Louise has kept in contact with this pastor and his wife, offering wise counsel when decisions had to be made. For Louise, this will be a continuing ministry until God releases her.

To a young man, newly married, who had ceased attending church, Louise wrote a motherly letter, praising him for the way he had overcome tough situations as he grew up.

"How proud I am of you," she wrote, "and of the way you allow God to help and use you. I have thanked God for you, and have prayed for you through the years."

Then she wrote of his new life, away from the home of his godly grandfather, setting up his new home. She reminded him of the importance of making right choices, and added, "There are a good number of young married people in our church whom God is depending on to take over leadership and responsibility. Could it be that He is depending on you? Please talk to Him definitely about these truths. I love you, Tom."

Strong men were not ashamed to listen to Louise. Her advice came straight from God and His word. There was one to whom Louise reached out when tragedy threatened to destroy him. He wanted to be a Christian. Then his wife ran away with another man. Rage possessed him. He wanted only to get even with the man who had done this to him.

With deep concern Louise wrote, "You are not forgotten, son. My heart aches to help you find yourself. I am praying much for you. Do you realize that Jesus, too, prays for your deliverance? Right now, He is making intercession at the throne of God for you.

"You want to be a good man, I know. In many ways you are. God put good stuff in you when He made you. . . . Your trouble is you have made yourself your God. . . . God cannot live in an unholy place, and you cannot live a life of purity and power with the old beast of carnality within. . . . Look at Peter in the Bible. He boasted that he was ready to die for Jesus, then denied he ever knew Him. But look again at Peter after Pentecost. He was bold for Christ.

"Turn yourself over to God completely. You just ride along and leave the driving all to Him. God will change you like He changed Simon Peter, and our friend, Harley, and like He changed me."

The man listened. Today, he is a redeemed wonder for God.

Harley was a man who often crossed to the opposite side of the street to avoid meeting Louise. She pursued him in prayer. Harley suffered from a severe skin disorder on his hands. The skin peeled off, leaving his hands cracked and bleeding. Doctors were baffled.

Louise prayed healing into Harley's hands and into his soul.

Radames was another of Louise's spiritual trophies. He wrote, "I will always remember a phone call from you, when you read to me the story of the prodigal son and said it sounded a lot like me. I agreed. I knew the Lord was calling me back to Him. Two or three weeks before Easter I re-dedicated my life to the Lord Jesus Christ. I thank God for you and the way God used you to minister to me."

District superintendents, pastors, lay Christians, adults, and children continually make their way to Louise's door. At times, Buena King steps in, with a kind but firm, "Not now. Mrs. Chapman is resting. Come back later."

Louise always gives special attention to the children who come to Casa Robles. She wants to greet each one personally. She prays for them. "I love the children," Louise said, as a group of them left her house. "They have such vast potential for God. From these little ones will come the great spiritual leaders of our church tomorrow. We must not let Satan get hold of them."

Baby churches also draw Louise Chapman's love and concern. Throughout her ministry in Africa and in the States, Louise has periodically adopted a struggling little church, writing, praying long hours for them, giving small donations to help them get started. She never coddles, but encourages them to get into the harness and grow strong in the Lord.

Eagle Rock Church of the Nazarene in Los Angeles is one of her latest "children."

Eagle Rock was an old church—67 years—that had fallen on hard times in recent years. Louise learned of the young pastor who was trying to revive the church, while having to work full-time. He was discouraged and nearly ready to quit when God told Louise to adopt Eagle Rock.

Alabaster Offering time was coming. Louise produced a yard-long clear plastic tube, just wide enough to hold quarters. She gave a little pep talk to the church and Sunday School, urging the children to bring in their quarters and fill the tube for Alabaster.

The novelty of the idea captured the children. They knew each one could put at least one quarter in the tube. Louise urged the pastor to challenge the church at each service to fill their Alabaster boxes. The people brought the largest Alabaster Offering they had ever given.

Before they had time to relax, Louise wrote them a pre-Easter letter reporting the wonderful things happening in the world today—the great opportunities opening up for the gospel in Russia, Berlin, Cambodia, Madagascar.

"All around the world we are pushing forward with banners waving," she wrote. Then she shifted to a personal note: "I was glad to hear, and very proud of you, whom I consider my adopted church, that last year you grew spiritually and handled your local, district, and general budgets well. God richly blessed every one of you. Now it is time for this year's report. I'm glad you are planning to send your pastor to the district assembly with a good report and all budgets paid.

"Eagle Rock is 67 years old this year. I'm sure you will all march at Easter. Every child is important. Ask Jesus how much He can help you bring. Every member and friend has a chance to participate in this great Investment Plan. Jesus is leading us. Bring in the last penny needed to pay your share in full. Here is my check to help you . . ."

Louise's enthusiasm and assurance left no room for "dead wood" Christians. People felt compelled to get in and boost the pastor, the church, and the district.

When Pasadena College moved from its campus in Pasadena, Calif., to San Diego, Louise was concerned lest this property, sacred to God's work for so many years, should fall into the hands of secular interests. She prayed for God to bring a Christian group to occupy it.

The bid of the fledgling U.S. Center for World Mission, led by Dr. Donald McGavran and Dr. Ralph Winter, to take on the campus and a huge debt, tickled Louise. It's just the way God has worked for me, she thought, David tackling Goliath. And Louise began to boost the little group in prayer. When their first letter came out challenging millions of people of every denomination to give a one-time gift of $15.00 and promise to pray for the new venture, she was delighted. "This is so right!" she exclaimed. "No church will face a hardship locally if their members give just $15.00 to help this group get started."

She wrote for packets of their brochure and sent them to hundreds of her friends, urging them to participate. She prayed with the leaders through the critical hours when it looked as though the project was going to fall. She rejoiced with them when God brought them through.

When they sent out their final call for 8,000 people or groups each to pay the last $1,000, she was momentarily stopped. This was different. Were they becoming like all the other money-raising groups across the country, invading other churches for big sums?

She wrote to Dr. Ralph Winter in her usual fashion: Praise first—"The Lord is with thee thou mighty [men] of valor. It is beautiful the way God has led and used you up to this present time in making such heavy property payments with such small donations. Had it not been God's plan you could never have come where you are today.

"When I first heard of the new attempt to find 8,000 people or groups each to pay the last $1,000 and then pay off the whole debt . . . I felt it was a sensible and workable plan. I was excited. Then I remembered how God gave you the $15.00 plan so thousands would pray . . . it seemed like 'changing horses in the middle of the stream' and troubled me. I was reminded then, of the great amount of precious money that had to be used for interest . . . I felt this was God's explanation to me and I was personally satisfied . . . but 8,000 is a lot of people. You do need the prayers of many more thousands. As I prayed about this, God gave me this message: 'Man of God . . . the Lord is able to give [you] much more than this' (2 Chron. 25:9). To me it was an answer to all my questions. I thought this scripture and my experience as I prayed might be an encouragement to you. I have notified the U.S. Center of World Mission that by His help I will be one of the needed 8,000. God bless you."

Throughout her lifetime, from time to time God has given Louise a fellow pilgrim on the journey, who shares her deepest prayer concerns. In Africa, she found prayer companions in Alice Kumalo and one or two other Swazi women of mighty faith. In America, there have been others. From the day that God decreed Louise should not return to Africa, she found such a person in Mrs. Gideon Williamson. They were persons of like spirit, knowing how to search the Word for assurance and how to fast and hold on in prayer for answers to great needs.

Recalling those times, Mrs. Williamson said, "We enjoyed visiting together, but our deepest fellowship was shared when we were concentrating in prayer on the same subject, often across miles, and at the same hour of the clock. Our spirits blended . . . we both felt we must have the support of scripture. Neither of us could imagine praying for anything not backed by the Word of God. When we had that, we would hang on until God answered. If we found a prayer promise that applied to the need, we claimed anything in the name of God. Sometimes we searched for many days before a Word was quickened to us and we knew God was speaking on the subject of our concern."

Mrs. Williamson added, "I was impressed by Louise's passion to determine God's will and do it, however impossible it looked to human eyes. She never undertook anything without knowing it was God's will."

10

"God's Pet" Receives Her Last Assignment

"God's Pet!" Strange title for one to whom God gave such tough assignments, and whom He caused to walk through such deep waters of tragedy and catastrophe. Yet Louise felt at one time that she must be one of God's pets, because He loved her so much and did so many wonderful things for her in answer to prayer. She was sure God couldn't possibly love anyone else as much as He loved her.

"God's Pet"—because she had found the depths of total surrender to the will of God that rested on bedrock. She knew, with Paul, that "neither death nor life, neither angels nor demons, neither the present nor the future, nor any powers, neither height nor depth, nor anything else in all creation, will be able to separate us from the love of God" (Rom. 8:38-39, NIV).

One would think that for someone who turned 100 years old on October 9, 1992, God might say, "Relax now and take your rest," but not so.

Only a short time ago, Louise Chapman wrote with deep emotion, "Many of our Christians have not tarried until they were filled with the Holy Spirit and power. Much of my work and prayers are centered on this group. Oh, how we need an outpouring of the Holy Spirit! Once in NNC I saw God sweep through the college and sanctify people like He did on the Day of Pentecost. Out in Africa, after 10 days of fasting and prayer, God came in mighty power. Preachers were sanctified, Bible school students and girls in our home were transformed by new cleansing and power . . . nearly every Christian at Schmelzenbach Memorial moved into holiness.

"I keep advertising this glorious provision for Christians. It is God's answer for the church."

At an age to which most of us do not expect to live, God has given Louise Chapman a new assignment. It could be her last, though with God and Louise, one can never be sure.

In 1988 God told Louise He wanted her to raise a million dollars annually for World Mission Radio, the money to be used to finance new programs in the opening countries of Eastern Europe, and to establish Communication Training Centers in the six Nazarene world regions. There the citizens of those countries could be trained to create programs and broadcast them, resulting eventually in the people in each area supporting these training areas themselves.

It is a stupendous assignment. How could one homebound woman hope to gather a million dollars? To make it more challenging, Satan, or circumstances, have created an economic slowdown in many countries of the world. What we do, we must do by faith. How else, anyway?

In a plea in the *Herald of Holiness* recently, Louise wrote, "Today is the day of radio. Tomorrow it will be some new and different tool. Today is ours to use. Who can know what tomorrow will bring?"

In her own methodical pattern, Louise worked out a way to accomplish the goal God has given her.

"Get 40,000 people to give just $25.00 a year to World Mission Radio and it will be done.

"Let this be a solemn promise between each donor and God."

Louise suggested a surprising source: "I see two areas of our church where we are allowing tremendous amounts of talent to lie untouched. One of these untapped areas is our thousands of children. It would demand wise leadership and hard work, but it would pay rich dividends in the future. Remember Dr. J. B. Chapman's story about raising our own kittens in the mill? We need to train our children to give for world needs, if we want them to respond when they are adults.

"Our children could share in the million dollars annually for World Mission Radio by promising to give $1.00 a year, or perhaps $5.00 for older children.

"The other area of wasted talent is our growing group of senior adults. What a tremendous power and talent is being lost to the church among our senior adults! Has any ministry of the church tried to give these good people a special and important assignment for Christ?

"I'd like to see an army of our senior members giving $25.00 a year for World Mission Radio for its 40th anniversary in 1993. I've even dreamed bigger dreams. After 1993, the seniors might be glad to sponsor praying for and financing World Mission Radio each year until God gets people in other countries trained to support their own radio work.

"Thousands of our senior citizens are already prayer intercessors. They have more time than some. They know how to pray. Most of them could give $25,00 a year without hardship."

Louise's burden was picked up by the NWMS. They challenged friends to give $100 for World Mission Radio by Louise's birthday in October 1992. If 3,000 friends responded, their gifts, added to the $700,000 already given, would bring in the first million for World Mission Radio.

Louise's plan to enlist the senior adults and the children would bring in the same amount in future years.

As a personal project, Louise is praying that at least 100 business men or women will give $1,000 in 1993 to help provide the Communication Training Centers, which will be named in her honor.

Louise ended her plea for radio with a prayer: "Lord, anoint my eyes that I may see those over-ripened fields and the awful destruction that will come if the storm hits before the crop is gathered in . . . touch my heart, O my God, until I feel the awful emptiness and total lostness of mankind without Christ . . ."

Does God ever stop giving new challenges to His obedient children? Evidently not. Even as this book was being prepared, Louise reported that God had spoken to her saying, "I want all the money you have."

He reminded her of the $4,000 she had saved to pay for any last illness she might have "when she got old."

"Why, sure, Lord," Louise cheerfully responded. "Everything I have is Yours—You know that."

She pulled out her checkbook to write a check for $4,000. God said, "I want that dollar you have in your purse."

"That's Yours too," Louise responded.

Telling of it afterward, she said with a gleeful laugh, "I feel so free!"

Thoughts of her coming birthday on October 9 brought excitement—not for herself but for God's latest assignment. Would the million dollar goal be reached by then? Louise doubled her efforts in prayer and letters to friends.

Then, in July 1992, just three months before her 100th birthday, Louise learned that she had inoperable cancer. She was incredulous, "At my age?" she exclaimed. "Who would ever have expected such a thing!"

Her doctor assured her that he felt she would see her 100th birthday. Confidently, Louise sent friends to buy her a new dress for the occasion.

"I'll hold on till my birthday," she said, "then I'm just going to hang loose and let God do whatever He pleases."

Dr. Nina Gunter, NWMS director, and the General NWMS Council went ahead with their plans for a birthday celebration at Casa Robles. As September lengthened, Louise's strength waned. Anxious friends watched and prayed.

On Saturday, October 3, Juliet Ndzmandze arrived from Swaziland to share in the celebration. She knelt beside Louise's bed, clasped her hand, and murmured "Mama Dulile."

It was like a resurrection! Louise was suddenly vibrant with life. She visited with friends, rode around the Casa Robles grounds in her wheelchair, and went to the weekly prayer meeting on Thursday morning.

On October 9, pink and white balloons hung everywhere in the trees and shrubs at Casa Robles.

Louise was taken to the Pavilion and seated under the canopy. Two hundred and fifty or more friends gathered around to celebrate the great day.

Overhead a small plane circled, trailing a banner that said "Happy 100th Birthday, Dr. Chapman."

General Superintendent Jerald D. Johnson spoke of his appreciation for Louise and her ministry. At the close of his remarks, he presented Louise with a plaque from the Board of General Superintendents.

In response, Louise said, "I never was afraid of the general superintendents. They were friends and coworkers. Once I took a project to them that I felt God wanted the NWMS to do. They turned me down, saying it would smash the General Budget to pieces. I said, 'Let 'er smash! This is from God.' And I was right!"

Dr. Phyllis Perkins, professor of Nazarene Bible College, brought words of praise and appreciation and announced that in Louise Chapman's honor, the Louise Robinson Chapman Scholarship Fund was being established at the Bible college to assist women students preparing for missionary or pastoral service.

Dr. Mary Scott described the close fellowship they had shared in their 17 years as coworkers in the general NWMS leadership. As Mary quoted one of the NWMS theme choruses, "Forward! Forward! Never to settle down . . . ," Louise raised her arms and cried, "Yes! Never settle down. Go forward!"

Marti Jordick, now confined to a wheelchair, spoke with deep feeling of Louise's ministry to her in her struggle to get free from the habits that bound her. When Marti finished, Louise exclaimed, "I fought the devil personally for that girl's soul! I felt I was standing on the edge of the earth hanging on to Marti. I told the devil he could have everything else, but he could not touch Marti's soul. Marti belonged to Jesus. I fought him with all my strength until God and I won the battle."

With tears, Louise's niece, Sandra, said, "I am a product of her prayers. I could go to Louise with any need and know it was private—between her and God. I knew she would now touch God's glory."

Juliet Ndzmandze saluted Louise with the Swazi flag—a ceremony reserved only for the Swazi royal family, but Juliet explained, "As a 'Daughter of the Heavenly King' Louise was worthy of this honor."

Indeed, the king of Swaziland chose to honor Louise by having his secretary provide the travel documents quickly for Juliet to come, and then presented Juliet with a new outfit to wear to the birthday celebration.

"Swaziland loves you, Mother Dulile," Juliet said. "You taught us to pray. You were the matron/preacher to hundreds of Swazi girls—a great soul. You were not an argumentative woman—you were a man among men (the highest compliment a woman could receive in Swaziland)—a teacher to many—a specialist for broken bones—mighty in prayer.

"I remember your face and my mother's face shone with glory from heaven. Many souls were won to Christ through you.

"Each district in Swaziland sends $100 to our mother and grandmother for World Mission Radio.

"The Swaziland church sent me a message asking us to pray that your mantle of faith and intercession will fall upon them."

Louise responded, "When I saw that magnificent check it just made me cry." Then she raised her hands in emphasis, exclaiming, "We are all in this together. Everyone stand in his place round about the camp.

"'Forward! Forward! Never to settle down . . .' That's the only way it can be done! Let it be 1992!"

The breadth of Louise's ministry in recent years was revealed as 12-year-old Kelly Akhbari spoke: "I met Dr. Chapman first in reading her book *Africa, O Africa*. I told my mother I had to meet that woman. She brought me to Casa Robles. We talked. Mrs. Chapman prayed for me. It was the longest prayer I ever heard. Since that day she has written me letters, and once she sent me money. We are friends."

Dr. Nina Gunter and Russell Bredholt presented Louise with a large card bearing the names of all who have given to the special $160,000 offering for World Mission Radio Leadership Training Centers.

Ray Hendrix, director of Communications, read a letter stating that a total of $834,000 had come in thus far for World Mission Radio.

After every greeting, Louise offered a challenge. At one point she exclaimed, "Holiness changes hearts. It makes us what we are not—patient, kind, humble. All we need is God, the wonderful power of God!

"O Lord, clothe them in Thy glory. Clothe every one of them with glory. No matter if they get nothing else."

She looked at the friends grouped around her. "I'm expecting God to work in you—all of you," she said earnestly. "I pray for a holiness church—a holiness crowd. People who look, act like, and talk like God. Don't ever retire! I will never retire until the day God takes me home. Ask God for something to do. Nobody can keep us from God—from praying."

To the listeners it seemed as though Louise was reaching out for someone to take up the task she was soon to lay down.

After five hours, the planned "30-minute program" ended and a radiant Louise Chapman was taken to her home to rest, though rest became increasingly difficult as friends streamed by to express personal good wishes to her.

Where can the story of this great woman of God end? Who can say?

Perhaps one day we will hear of another "impossible" assignment that God has given "His Pet," and Louise will be challenging us to new and higher achievements in God's kingdom.

Louise Chapman exhorting at her 100th birthday celebration, October 9, 1992

Louise Chapman and Juliet Ndzmandze at her 100th birthday celebration